Christians today face an arra about spiritual gifts. In this co bines faithful biblical scholarsl ...... for the Word of God. His arguments are clear, charitable, and compelling. I highly recommend it.

R. Albert Mohler Jr., president
The Southern Baptist Theological Seminary

Tom Schreiner has written a well-balanced and compelling book on a qualified view of "cessationism." His discussions are filled with solid biblical interpretation, biblical logic, wisdom, and an irenic spirit. This is quite a feat, since the subject matter is so debated among evangelicals. Even those who might disagree with Schreiner's views will find his discussions profitable to read. I commend this reliable book. I will recommend it to others.

G. K. Beale, professor of
New Testament and Biblical Theology
Westminster Theological Seminary

In *Spiritual Gifts: What They Are & Why They Matter*, not only does Tom Schreiner build a convincing case for the cessationist position, he shows us how to address controversies in the church with humble charity, biblical clarity, and theological conviction. This book sweeps away misconceptions, upholds the sufficiency of Scripture, and drives us to reflect again on the biblical text. Even those who don't fully agree will profit from this work.

John Folmar, senior pastor
United Christian Church of Dubai (UAE)

SPIRITUAL GIFTS

What They Are & Why They Matter

SPIRITUAL GIFTS

What They Are & Why They Matter

THOMAS R. SCHREINER

B&H

PUBLISHING GROUP

NASHVILLE, TENNESSEE

Published by B&H Publishing Group
Nashville, Tennessee

Cover design and illustration by Ligia Teodosiu.

Dewey Decimal Classification: 234.13
Subject Heading: CHRISTIANITY \ SPIRITUAL GIFTS \
SPIRITUAL LIFE

1 2 3 4 5 6 7 • 22 21 20 19 18

To Wayne Grudem, John Piper, and Sam Storms.
Beloved friends and coworkers in the gospel of Christ

Acknowledgments

I would never have written this book if John Kimbell, the preaching pastor at Clifton Baptist Church, had not asked me to speak on spiritual gifts at the Clifton men's retreat. Even after speaking on the issue, I don't think I would have written this book without the encouragement of my dear friend (and my next-door neighbor) and colleague, Oren Martin. He kept telling me to write this book, and I won't blame him if it has a bad reception! I also tried out the material in this book at Founders Baptist Church in Spring, Texas. Richard Caldwell, the preaching pastor, has been a wonderful friend and a pastor whom I have now known for many years. I am thankful to B&H Publishing Group and Devin Maddox and Taylor Combs for their enthusiastic support and encouragement for writing this book. Another dear friend, who is a continuationist, Chris Bruno, read the manuscript and made some helpful observations. One of my PhD students, who is also a continuationist, Jarrett Ford, read the manuscript, challenging me at a number of points. I didn't convince him, and he didn't convince me, but I am thankful for Jarrett's careful reading, which helped me sharpen my argument. Jarrett also chased down some details in the footnotes for which I am thankful. I am also grateful to another PhD student, Richard Blaylock, who read the manuscript carefully, saving me from some errors. He also made a number of comments which helped me improve the argument. I also benefited from Richard's essay on prophecy, which will I hope be accepted for publication soon. Richard also assisted me by verifying some of the footnotes.

Contents

Introduction

I wanted to write a small book on spiritual gifts because I support a position called "cessationism"—at least, it is a kind of cessationism.[1] Still, this book isn't only about cessationism. I also sketch in a theology of spiritual gifts. I hope this part of the book won't be ignored, for we are all prone to concentrate on controversies. In other words, I hope readers don't skip the other chapters and only read what I have written about cessationism. I suppose some readers will do that anyway, but I think they will lose some perspective on the book as a whole, and may therefore read what I say from a distorted standpoint.

Before embarking on the journey, I want to say some personal things. The first is, *I could be mistaken in arguing for cessationism*. The matter isn't simple to resolve. If it were entirely clear, faithful believers would not come to different points of view. Fortunately, one's theology and perspective on spiritual

---

[1] The most concise definition of cessationism is the belief that certain spiritual gifts in the New Testament—namely the more miraculous gifts—have ceased. This will be unpacked in greater detail throughout the book.

1

gifts isn't a first-order issue. We are not discussing the Trinity or the person of Christ or justification by faith.

At the same time, our understanding of spiritual gifts is important because churches have to decide whether the gifts will be exercised in the congregation. In my circles people often say they are open but cautious about the spiritual gifts, but most who hold this stance don't actually practice the spiritual gifts. What I see less often is a defense of the idea that a number of the spiritual gifts have ceased. Often cessationist churches don't talk about the gifts, and many in such churches aren't sure what they should think about spiritual gifts.

We should be instructed about the gifts, for Paul said in 1 Corinthians 12:1, "Now concerning spiritual gifts: brothers and sisters, I do not want you to be unaware." Some say they are tired of spiritual gifts since there has been significant controversy over them. They don't want to hear about the subject anymore. They have heard so much about them, or argued so long over them that they no longer care. But Paul says knowing the truth about spiritual gifts is important. He doesn't want us to be ignorant about spiritual gifts. So, our study does matter. It is part of God's revealed Word that we should know.

I have hesitated to write this little book because I don't want to be polemical and divisive. How wearisome and tiring it is to engage in arguments, especially with those whom we love and cherish! The spirit in some discussions has turned many away from the matter of spiritual gifts altogether. Sometimes faithful, Bible-believing Christians have a way of shutting down the voices of those with whom we disagree, even on second- and third-order issues. It is more comfortable for all of us to associate with those who agree with us. Sometimes we harshly criticize those who disagree, but what we need instead is loving and charitable discussion. Respectful discussions on matters where there is disagreement are helpful. Our culture is more and more polarized, and it seems that many can't tolerate those who disagree with them on any matter. They want to live in a space free from any dissenting voices. As believers, we should not follow the same pattern. Strong convictions are good, but we need discriminating judgment so that we don't fall into the error of thinking that every issue is of equal importance. As evangelicals we have to beware of false teaching, but we also have to be on guard against a rigid fundamentalism that doesn't tolerate disagreements. The inability to tolerate some disagreement isn't only found in political circles; we can fall into the same error as evangelicals.

Some of my beloved friends and teachers disagree with me on this issue, including John Piper, Wayne Grudem, and Sam Storms. I have enormous respect and love for each of these men, and I have dedicated this book to them to register my respect and admiration for each one. They have all influenced me in significant ways, especially John Piper, who was my pastor for eleven years. Even though I disagree with them on the matter before us, I would happily be a member of the churches they attend and pastor.

One of the books that convinced me to be a continuationist for some years was written by D. A. Carson,[2] and Carson's writings have shaped me significantly in many additional ways over the years. I concede up front that those who differ from me may see things more clearly than I.

My intention isn't to write an in-depth and scholarly treatment on the matter of spiritual gifts. This is a short book for anyone who wants to gain more knowledge of spiritual gifts. My intention isn't to interact in detail with different points of view, nor am I trying to summarize what other scholars say on spiritual gifts. Those who know the writings of Grudem, Storms, and Carson will recognize that here and there that I am interacting with their views, but my purpose isn't to chronicle other views; rather, I aim to present a brief defense of my own. My desire is that this short, relatively nontechnical book could be given to people who want to read a brief discussion on spiritual gifts. The chapters, then, are relatively small, amenable to reading in a short period of time.

---

[2] D. A. Carson, *Showing the Spirit: A Theological Exposition of 1 Corinthians 12–14* (Grand Rapids, MI: Baker, 1987).

Discussion Questions

1. What is your personal history with spiritual gifts?

2. Which word is more associated in your mind with spiritual gifts: *chaos* or *order*? *Personal* or *corporate*?

3. Why is it important to remember that a theology of spiritual gifts is not a first-order issue (p. 2)?

Chapter One

Strengths and Weaknesses of the Charismatic Movement

J. I. Packer notes several strengths and weaknesses of the charismatic movement.[1] I believe Packer's words are theologically helpful and pastorally wise. They help set a context for our study of the gifts, which we wouldn't be talking about apart from the charismatic movement. I expand briefly on Packer's observations.

Positive: What We Can Learn from Charismatics

1. "*Spirit-Empowered Living.* Emphasis is laid on the need to be filled with the Spirit and to be living a life that one way or

---

[1] J. I. Packer, *Keep in Step with the Spirit: Finding Fullness in Our Walk with God*, revised and enlarged (Grand Rapids: Baker, 2005).

another displays the Spirit's power."[2] Sometimes we as evangelicals tend to ignore the Holy Spirit, and charismatics remind us about the third person of the Trinity and the need to be filled with the Spirit.

2. "*Emotion Finding Expression.* There is an emotional element in the makeup of each human individual, which calls to be expressed in any genuine appreciation and welcoming of another's love, whether it be the love of a friend or a spouse or the love of God in Christ. Charismatics understand this, and their provision for exuberance of sight, sound, and movement in corporate worship caters to it."[3] Right doctrine is important, but so is our experience with God. Sometimes we stress right thinking but neglect other dimensions of what it means to be human.

3. "*Prayerfulness.* Charismatics stress the need to cultivate an ardent, constant, wholehearted habit of prayer."[4] How crucial as Christians it is to be in communion with God, and charismatics remind us of our personal relationship with God.

4. "*Every-Heart Involvement in the Worship of God.* Charismatics . . . insist that all Christians must be personally active in the church's worship."[5] Worship isn't the exclusive province of leaders, and charismatics rightly stress every-member

---

[2] Ibid., 151. All the italics in the quotations are from Packer.
[3] Ibid.
[4] Ibid.
[5] Ibid., 152.

8

worship. The body as a whole ministers to itself, and charismatics capture this biblical truth.

5. *"Missionary Zeal."*[6] Charismatics long to see others converted and saved to the ends of the earth. The Pentecostal/charismatic movement is worldwide the largest Christian movement.

6. *"Small-Group Ministry.* Like John Wesley, who organized the Methodist Societies round the weekly class meeting of twelve members under their class leader, charismatics know the potential of group."[7] The usefulness of smaller group meetings has been recognized by believers, as small group ministry has expanded.

7. *"Communal Living."*[8] Charismatics extend the sense of family in churches.

8. *"Joyfulness.* At the risk of sounding naïve, Pollyannaish, and smug, they insist that Christians should rejoice and praise God at all times and in all places, and their commitment to joy is often writ large on their faces, just as it shines bright in their behavior."[9] There is an openness to the Spirit and child-like trust, joy and humility, which is refreshing in this cynical world.

---

[6] Ibid., 153.
[7] Ibid.
[8] Ibid., 154.
[9] Ibid., 152.

9. *Real Belief in Satan and the Demonic.*[10] Many Christians say they believe in Satan, but charismatics take the demonic seriously.

10. *Real Belief in the Miraculous.* We still believe that God can do miracles, but sometimes we live like Deists, as if God weren't active at all in the world. Charismatics don't make that mistake.

Negative: Weaknesses in the Charismatic Movement

1. "*Elitism.* In any movement in which significant-seeming things go on, the sense of being a spiritual aristocracy, the feeling that 'we are the people who really count,' always threatens at gut level, and verbal disclaimers of this syndrome do not always suffice to keep it at bay."[11] Interestingly, this is the same problem we see in 1 Corinthians where those who spoke in tongues saw themselves as spiritually superior.

2. "*Sectarianism.* The absorbing intensity of charismatic fellowship, countrywide and worldwide, can produce a damaging insularity whereby charismatics limit themselves to reading charismatic books, hearing charismatic speakers, fellowshiping with other charismatics, and backing charismatic causes."[12]

---

[10] These last two strengths are not included in Packer's work.
[11] Ibid., 155.
[12] Ibid.

Charismatics are sometimes incredibly narrow so that there is little willingness to learn from other branches of Christendom.

3. "*Anti-intellectualism.* Charismatic preoccupation with experience observably inhibits the long, hard theological and ethical reflection for which the New Testament letters so plainly calls."[13] The emphasis on emotions can slight and denigrate the importance of careful thought. Careful interpretation of Scripture and orthodox theology are too often ignored. In scholarly charismatic circles the inerrancy of Scripture is denied quite often, and in popular circles people may rely on revelations from God for their daily life, in effect denying the sufficiency of Scripture.

4. "*Illuminism.* Sincere but deluded claims to direct divine revelation have been made in the church since the days of the Colossians heretic(s) and the Gnosticizers whose defection called forth 1 John, and since Satan keeps pace with God, they will no doubt recur till the Lord returns. At this point the charismatic movement, with its stress on the Spirit's personal leading and the revival of revelations via prophecy, is clearly vulnerable."[14] Some claim God speaks directly to them, and they aren't open to any correction or questioning of such claims. The focus on contemporary revelation may compromise or even contradict the teaching of Scripture.

---

[13] Ibid., 156.
[14] Ibid.

5. "*Charismania.* This is Edward D. O'Connor's word for the habit of mind that measures spiritual health, growth, and maturity by the number and impressiveness of people's gifts, and spiritual power by public charismatic manifestation."[15] In practice 1 Corinthians 13—where our spiritual life is measured by our love for others—may be ignored.

6. "*Super-supernaturalism.* Charismatic thinking tends to treat glossolalia in which the mind and tongue are deliberately and systematically disassociated, as the paradigm case of spiritual activity, and to expect all God's work in and around his children to involve similar discontinuity with the ordinary regularities of the created world."[16] Most of life is lived in the ordinary. We don't live miracle-a-minute lives. The most important moments in our lives are often invisible to others and even to us.

7. "*Eudaemonism.* I use this word for the belief that God means to spend our time in this fallen world feeling well and in a state of euphoria based on that fact. Charismatics might deprecate so stark a statement, but the regular and expected projection of euphoria from their platforms and pulpits, plus their standard theology of healing, show that the assumption is there."[17] Many charismatics (though not all!) throughout the

---

[15] Ibid., 156.
[16] Ibid., 157.
[17] Ibid.

world espouse the health and wealth gospel, and it is clearly the most popular false gospel in the world. When we read the New Testament, it is apparent that God often calls upon his people to suffer, and the role of suffering in the Christian life is often neglected among charismatics.

8. *"Demon Obsession."*[18] Some see demons everywhere, and identify every sin with a demon. Also, the emphasis on "territorial spirits" in some circles is off-center and often quite speculative.

9. *"Conformism.* Peer pressure to perform (hands raised, hands outstretched, glossolalia, prophecy) is strong in charismatic circles."[19] People may feel compelled to have the same spiritual experiences, and we may measure how spiritual someone is by the emotions expressed or by physical movements.

10. *Experience Centered.*[20] A danger in the charismatic movement and in evangelicalism generally is a focus on experience so that experience takes precedence over and trumps Scripture. Powerful experiences of God are a gift of God, but Scripture must play a foundational role so that experience is not accepted as self-authenticating. Experience is subordinate to Scripture so that experiences do not become the arbiter of what is permitted. Instead, Scripture is the final authority

---

[18] Ibid., 158.

[19] Ibid., 157.

[20] This last weakness is not included in Packer's work.

and experiences are only to be accepted if they accord with Scripture.

The charismatic movement has both strengths and weaknesses, areas where they challenge non-charismatic churches, and areas where they could learn from traditional churches. For a genuine understanding of the gifts, we must turn to the Scriptures, and that is our next task.

Discussion Questions

1. Which of the strengths of the charismatic movement stood out to you? Which of the weaknesses?

2. If you don't come from a charismatic background, what can you learn from your brothers and sisters who do?

3. If you do come from a charismatic background, what can you learn from your brothers and sisters who do not?

Chapter Two

Defining Spiritual Gifts

Terminology

When we think of spiritual gifts, it is helpful to think about what spiritual gifts are. In this chapter, I offer definitions for the spiritual gifts found in the Scriptures.

Paul uses various words to denote spiritual gifts. For instance, we find the word *pneumatika* (1 Cor. 12:1; 14:1), and in the latter verse it is translated, "spiritual gifts." The word *pneuma* in the plural also designates spiritual gifts. The believers in Corinth are "zealous for spiritual gifts (*pneumatōn*)" (1 Cor. 14:12). And "the spiritual gifts (*pneumata*) of the prophets are subject to the prophets" (1 Cor. 14:32).[1] Spiritual gifts are also identified as a

---

[1] My translation.

"manifestation of the Spirit" (*phanerōsis tou pneumatos*, 1 Cor. 12:7). These various terms all stress the *spirituality* of gifts, showing that they come from the Holy Spirit, and since the gifts come from the Holy Spirit they are supernatural.

Other terms emphasize that we are given *gifts*. For instance, Paul uses the term *charismata* (1 Cor. 12:4; 12:31; Rom. 12:6) to designate the gifts. In Ephesians 4:7 the word "grace" (*charis*) is used for the spiritual gifts given to believers. In the next verse (Eph. 4:8) we find the word "gifts" (*domata*). We learn from these terms that the spiritual abilities or activities (they are identified as "activities" [*energēmata*] in 1 Corinthians 12:6) are granted by God. They don't testify to native or inherent human potential but are *gifts* of God. In addition, the word "ministries" (*diakoniai*, 1 Cor. 12:5) shows that the gifts aren't designed to help oneself but are given to serve and build up others.

> *Spiritual gifts are gifts of grace granted by the Holy Spirit which are designed for the edification of the church.*

I would define spiritual gifts as gifts of grace granted by the Holy Spirit which are designed for the edification of the church.

Ken Berding argues that when Paul refers to spiritual gifts, he doesn't have in mind special abilities a person possesses. Instead, the gifts designate ministry functions and roles people are to fulfill.[2] Resolving this issue isn't the main purpose of this book, but a few comments should be made. Berding rightfully emphasizes that gifts are given to believers so that we will serve and minister to others; they don't focus on our own abilities. It does seem to me, however, that ministry roles and abilities are not enemies but friends. Gifts like prophecy, teaching, tongues, etc., seem to be special abilities granted to believers, but the gifts are given for the edification of the church; they are used wrongly if we turn them into platforms for self-admiration.

Definitions

The chart on the following page lists the various spiritual gifts. Most agree that the list isn't exhaustive, though it is difficult to know what to add to the list. For instance, is musical ability a spiritual gift? It very well may be, and yet it is striking that Paul doesn't mention it. In any case, I will not speculate about other spiritual gifts that aren't listed but will restrict discussion to those named in the New Testament. Brief definitions will be given of the spiritual gifts with the exception of the gift of tongues and prophecy, which will be discussed later.

---

[2] See Kenneth Berding, *What Are Spiritual Gifts? Rethinking the Conventional View* (Grand Rapids, MI: Kregel, 2006).

Table of Spiritual Gifts in the New Testament[3]

Romans 12:6–8	1 Corinthians 12:7–10	1 Corinthians 12:28	Ephesians 4:11
Having gifts that differ according to the grace given to us	*To each is given the manifestation of the Spirit for the common good*	*And God has appointed in the church*	*And he gave*
		Apostles	Apostles
Prophecy	Prophecy	Prophets	Prophets
			Evangelists
	Ability to distinguish between spirits		
Teaching	Word of wisdom and word of knowledge	Teachers	Pastors and teachers
Exhorting			
	Working of miracles	Miracles	
	Gifts of healing	Gifts of healing	
Service		Helping	
Leading		Administrating	
	Various kinds of tongues	Various kinds of tongues	
	Interpretation of tongues		
Giving			
	Faith		
Mercy			

---

[3] The gifts aren't necessarily in the order in which they are listed in the biblical text.

Teaching

The first gifts mentioned in 1 Corinthians 12:8 are among the hardest to define. The "message of wisdom" and the "message of knowledge" ("word of wisdom" and "word of knowledge," literally) are difficult to pin down. In popular circles some have said that knowledge is academic understanding, while wisdom represents the ability to apply knowledge. Against this, there is no biblical justification for saying that knowledge is merely academic, as if knowledge in the Scriptures doesn't apply to everyday life. Others have maintained that the "word of knowledge" is a supernatural understanding of another person's sin, problem, disease, etc., so that one can discern if someone has cancer or is struggling with a particular sin. This latter definition, however, would seem to fit prophecy, which is already mentioned in this list, rather than knowledge.

I incline to the view that both "message of wisdom" and "message of knowledge" refer to the gift of teaching.[4] Paul doesn't mention teaching in the listing of the gifts in 1 Corinthians 12:8–10, and the gift is so important in Paul that it is included in every other list of spiritual gifts (1 Cor. 12:28–30; Rom. 12:6–8; Eph. 4:11). It seems unlikely that he would leave it out here, and other evidence points to a reference to teaching. For instance, in 1 Corinthians 1:18–2:16 wisdom is linked

---

[4] See Graham Houston, *Prophecy: A Gift for Today* (Downers Grove, IL: InterVarsity Press, 1989), 103–6.

with proclaiming Jesus Christ as the crucified one. Paul's use of "word" (*logos*), which we find in both the "message of wisdom" (*logos sophias*) and "message of knowledge" (*logos gnōseōs*) also points to teaching. Paul often refers to the message he preached as the "word of God" (Rom. 9:6; 1 Cor. 14:36; 2 Cor. 2:17; 4:2; Phil. 1:14; Col. 1:25; 1 Thess. 2:13; 1 Tim. 4:5; 2 Tim. 2:9; Titus 2:5), the "word of faith" (Rom. 10:8), the "word of truth" (2 Cor. 6:7; Col. 1:5; 2 Tim. 2:15; Eph. 1:13), "the word of the Lord" (1 Thess. 1:8; 2 Thess. 3:1), and the "word of life" (Phil. 2:16).[5] "Knowledge" in Paul is also linked with understanding, which accords well with the role teaching plays (cf. Rom. 15:14; Eph. 1:17; 4:13; Phil. 1:9–10; Col. 1:9–10; 2:2–4; 3:9–10; 1 Tim. 2:4; 2 Tim. 2:25; 3:7; Titus 1:1). All of this suggests that the *word* of wisdom and *word* of knowledge relates to teaching. Nor is it surprising that the expressions refer to one gift since the distinctions between the various gifts aren't always hard and fast.

I also suggest that 1 Corinthians 14:6 supports the idea that "knowledge" refers to teaching. "So now, brothers and sisters, if I come to you speaking in other tongues, how will I benefit you unless I speak to you with a revelation or knowledge or prophecy or teaching?" If we look at the verse closely, it seems that it has an ABAB pattern.

---

[5] All translations here are my own since English versions toggle between *word* and *message*, and I translated all as *word* for clarity.

A Revelation	A¹ Prophecy
B Knowledge	B¹ Teaching

Those who prophesy give a revelation, and those who teach provide knowledge, and so in both instances the consequence or result or product of the gift is listed first. If this is the case, when Paul speaks of knowledge coming to an end in 1 Corinthians 13:8, he refers to the gift of teaching. He acknowledges that those with the gift of teaching only "know in part" (1 Cor. 13:9), and full knowledge will only be given at the second coming (1 Cor. 13:12).

The gift of teaching is also noted in every other list of spiritual gifts (Rom. 12:7; 1 Cor. 12:28–29; Eph. 4:11). The importance of teaching is especially emphasized in the Pastoral Epistles (1 Tim. 1:10; 2:7, 12; 4:1, 6, 11, 13, 16; 5:17; 6:1–3; 2 Tim. 1:11; 3:10, 16; 4:3; Titus 1:9, 11; 2:1, 7, 10). Teachers expound, explicate, and unpack the Word of God, imparting instruction based on truth already revealed. It differs from prophecy in that it is not based on new revelation, and all elders should have this gift at least to some extent (1 Tim. 3:2; Titus 1:9).

Faith

The gift of faith (1 Cor. 12:8) can't be the same as saving faith since all believers have the latter. Thus, the gift of faith must refer to an extraordinary faith and vision for the future. It seems that Paul has this gift in mind when he speaks of a faith that "can move mountains" (1 Cor. 13:2). Perhaps the "prayer of faith" exercised by elders when one is sick (James 5:15) may also be an example of the gift of faith.

Healing and Miracles

The gifts of healing and miracles belong naturally together (1 Cor. 12:9–10). Some interpreters see significance in the plural: "gifts of healings" (*charismata iamatōn*), as if the gift isn't always available and that it may only be occasionally present. This may be true, although it is difficult to be certain since the plural is a thin reed upon which to base any conclusions. In any case, it seems difficult to speak in any meaningful sense of a *gift* of healing unless someone has the ability to heal with at least some regularity. Healing and miracles may overlap like wisdom and knowledge. Perhaps healing has to do with the healing of blindness, cancer, deafness, etc., while miracles could refer to exorcisms and nature miracles.

Distinguishing between Spirits

"Distinguishing between spirits" (1 Cor. 12:10) reflects the ability to discern between what is true and false. Perhaps we see this gift exercised when Paul becomes annoyed with the slave girl "who had a spirit by which she predicted the future"

(Acts 16:16). She commended Paul and Silas with the words, "These men, who are proclaiming to you the way of salvation, are the servants of the Most High God" (Acts 16:17). We might think that Paul would be pleased with these words since they were true, and even good advertising! But Paul discerned the evil spirit in her, and cast the demon out of her, understanding the true source of her power (Acts 16:18). Those who have the gift of discernment know the Scriptures well, and thus are particularly equipped "to test the spirits to see if they are from God" (1 John 4:1).

Helping

Paul also mentions the gift of "helping" (1 Cor. 12:28), which is one of the most practical gifts since it designates the many ways others can be assisted. The gift of helps is likely the same gift as the gift of "service" (*diakonia,* Rom. 12:7). Perhaps many who serve as deacons in churches have the gift of helps (cf. Phil. 1:1; 1 Tim. 3:8–11). Certainly, the gift isn't limited to deacons. In the history of the church there haven't been dramatic movements where people are ardently seeking the gift of helps! Still, it is one of the most useful and important gifts in the church, and no church would run effectively without it. Perhaps this is also the place to say that one can't refuse to offer practical help with the excuse that one doesn't have the gift of helps!

Administrating

We also find the gift of "administrating" (*kybernēseis*, 1 Cor. 12:28). The word in Proverbs has to do with guidance, with the direction one should travel in life (Prov. 1:5; 11:14; 24:6). The related word *kybernētēs* refers to pilots or captains of a boat (Ezek. 27:8, 27–28; Acts 27:11; Rev. 18:17). The gift of "leading" (*ho proistamenos,* Rom. 12:8) probably designates the same gift. Some see this gift in Romans as one who gives aid or cares for others, but in 1 Thessalonians 5:12 and in 1 Timothy 3:4–5; 5:17 the same term denotes leadership. One of the great needs of churches is godly and visionary leadership, and thus this gift plays a significant role in every church, for without direction churches become stagnant and rudderless.

Exhortation

The gift of exhortation (*paraklēsis*) is noted in Romans 12:7. This gift is rather broad and includes urging others to live righteously and showing pastoral care to the afflicted and distressed. Pastoral counseling belongs under the gift of exhortation, which is again one of the central ministries in churches as members care for one another in concrete ways. Preaching probably represents a combination of the gifts of teaching and exhortation. Some preachers excel more on the teaching end of the spectrum, while others excel more in exhortation. The best preachers blend these gifts together.

Giving

Another gift is "giving," which focuses on the giving of one's wealth and substance to assist others (Rom. 12:8). All believers are called upon to be generous and give, but some give in remarkable and unusual ways.

Mercy

Others have the gift of mercy (Rom. 12:8). Those who have the gift of mercy have a special capacity to minister to those who are hurting. All believers, of course, are to show compassion, but those with the gift of mercy have a special knack of attending to those who are in pain.

Evangelism

Some have the gift of evangelism (Eph. 4:11). Timothy is admonished to "do the work of an evangelist" (2 Tim. 4:5), which means proclaiming the good news of Jesus Christ to unbelievers. Every believer should be prepared to share the hope that is in them (1 Pet. 3:15), but some have a special gift of doing so. Church planters and missionaries in particular exercise this gift, but the gift may also be present in congregations where churches already exist.

Apostles

Paul also speaks of those who are gifted as apostles (1 Cor. 12:28–29; Eph. 4:11). In a narrow definition of the term, the gift of apostleship is restricted to those who have seen the risen Lord and have been commissioned by him (Mark 3:14; Luke 6:13; Acts 1:15–26). Clearly, the twelve apostles fit these qualifications, and Paul was called by Jesus Christ to be an apostle on the Damascus Road (Acts 9:1–19). Paul also saw the risen Lord at his conversion, as 1 Corinthians 9:1–2 makes clear: "Am I not free? Am I not an apostle? Have I not seen Jesus our Lord? Are you not my work in the Lord? If I am not an apostle to others, at least I am to you, because you are the seal of my apostleship in the Lord."

The apostolic circle isn't limited to the Twelve as the calling of Paul as an apostle makes clear. Furthermore, it is quite clear that James, the brother of Jesus, was also an apostle (Gal. 1:19). James's authoritative role in Jerusalem confirms his apostolic ministry, for he played a central role in the confirmation of Paul's gospel along with Peter and John (Gal. 2:1–10). James also gave the decisive last word at the Jerusalem Council, declaring that circumcision was not required for Gentiles to belong to the people of God (Acts 15:13–21). A few others may have also functioned as apostles in this technical sense, including Silas (Acts 15:32; 16:25) and Barnabas (Acts 4:36; 9:27; 14:4, 14).

The word in a less technical sense may represent pioneer missionaries, where those who are sent don't have the same authority as the apostles mentioned above. Andronicus and Junia are called apostles (Rom. 16:7), and they were probably a missionary couple who were well known for their work in spreading the gospel.

Conclusion

In this chapter I have endeavored to provide brief definitions of various gifts with the exception of tongues and prophecy. We have seen that there is remarkable variety in the gifts, and we can roughly divide them into two categories: gifts of speaking and gifts of serving (1 Pet. 4:11). Even this division isn't perfect since those who speak also serve those whom they address, and those who serve speak as they minister. Gifts of speaking include apostleship, prophecy, teaching, evangelism, exhortation, discerning spirits, speaking in tongues, and interpreting tongues. Gifts of service include leadership, helps, mercy, giving, faith, healing, and miracles. Our God is creative and infinitely wise, and his creativity and wisdom are reflected in the gifts he has given to the church of Jesus Christ.

Discussion Questions

1. How does this chapter define spiritual gifts?

2. Did you learn anything new from the definitions of the various spiritual gifts discussed in this chapter?

Chapter Three

Five Truths about Spiritual Gifts

In this chapter and the next we will investigate some important pastoral truths about spiritual gifts. We will look at five truths in this chapter and five more in the next.

The Lordship of Christ

We begin at the beginning—by noting that gifts are to be exercised under the lordship of Christ. Paul introduces the topic of spiritual gifts with the foundational truth of Jesus' lordship. "Now concerning spiritual gifts: brothers and sisters, I do not want you to be unaware. You know that when you were pagans, you used to be enticed and led astray by mute idols. Therefore I want you to know that no one speaking by the Spirit of God says, 'Jesus is cursed,' and no one can say, 'Jesus is Lord,' except by the Holy Spirit" (1 Cor. 12:1–3). The lordship of Christ is the criterion by which gifts are assessed. In other words, our gifts aren't a manifestation of ourselves or of our own abilities but are intended to communicate the truth that Jesus is Lord.

Ecstatic spiritual experiences aren't the center of our faith. When God gives us powerful experiences of his presence, we praise him for drawing near to us in such a gracious way. We should not and must not disregard such experiences with God.

The lordship of Christ is the criterion by which gifts are assessed.

At the same time, acknowledging Jesus as Lord in our hearts and in our lives is far more important than any stunning experience with the Lord.

Some people claim to have had amazing experiences, but they don't live under the lordship of Christ in their everyday lives. A person may claim to have staggering gifts, but if they aren't living in submission to the Lord Jesus Christ, they are failing in the most important area. Jesus warned us, "Not everyone who says to me, 'Lord, Lord,' will enter the kingdom of heaven, but only the one who does the will of my Father in heaven. On that day many will say to me, 'Lord, Lord, didn't we prophesy in your name, drive out demons in your name, and do many miracles in your name?' Then I will announce to them, 'I never knew you. Depart from me, you lawbreakers!'" (Matt. 7:21–23). Some (of course there are many significant exceptions!) in the charismatic world have a reputation for wonderful gifts, but then word gets out that they have been living contrary to the gospel in a significant way for years. We should question whether someone is exercising spiritual gifts in a way that is truly helpful if there is a pattern of hidden and blatant sin in his or her life. In a world where subjective experience is often used as the measure of our spiritual lives, Paul brings us back to the objective baseline of Christian experience—the lordship of Jesus.

Since Jesus is Lord, he can give the gifts as he wishes. Nowhere does Scripture teach that Christians have only one gift. Since Christ is Lord, he may give a person one gift, two gifts, or many gifts. Nothing in Scripture says that each person has *only* one gift, so we should leave this matter open, recognizing that God gives gifts sovereignly according to his will. He gives what he wills in order to accomplish his purposes. It is also possible that God would grant gifts of miracles, healings, and signs and wonders in a cutting edge missionary situation. I will argue later that such a situation isn't usual, and even on the mission field we can't expect such to happen, for it is the exception not the rule. Nonetheless, God may do as he pleases.

We see another dimension of living under Christ's lordship in 1 Peter 4:10–11: "Just as each one has received a gift, use it to serve others, as good stewards of the varied grace of God. If anyone speaks, let it be as one who speaks God's words; if anyone serves, let it be from the strength God provides, so that God may be glorified through Jesus Christ in everything. To him be the glory and the power forever and ever. Amen." If we are using our gifts to the glory of God, and we are living under Christ's lordship, we use our gifts to *serve* others. We sense an awesome responsibility before God to exercise our gifts as he desires. We serve under God's lordship when we are faithful in speaking so that we communicate the oracles of God. How amazing that God has given us the privilege to speak his word, which gives grace to others. Peter isn't just talking here about preaching sermons, for we all share God's word with others whether in small groups or one to one.

Finally, we don't have the strength and ability to serve in a way that pleases God on our own. The effectiveness of our spiritual gifts doesn't reside in us. We are conscious of our weakness and God's great strength. God in his mercy will not let us feel too greatly the effectiveness of our gifts so that we don't grow proud. He lets us feel weakness so that his strength shines through us. We recognize that we are unworthy servants, but at the same time we are grateful servants—for God has chosen to use us to help others in grace. And thus, as we serve under Christ's lordship, we give God the glory and praise in all that we do.

Think Reasonably about Your Gifts

The second truth is that we should not overestimate our godliness or effectiveness. Paul prefaces his discussion of spiritual gifts in Romans with these words in Romans 12:3: "For by the grace given to me, I tell everyone among you not to think of himself more highly than he should think. Instead, think sensibly, as God has distributed a measure of faith to each one." It is fitting here to quote the words of the great German commentator, Adolf Schlatter, on this verse. If you find his words hard to understand, I recommend that you read them over again slowly and thoughtfully, for what Schlatter says here is full of insight:

> Paul resists the danger that arises from the tempting power of the idea of equality. Each one wants to be and do like the others; no one wants to be less pious than the other. The danger that ensued from egalitarian endeavors[1] was not the paralyzing of faith, nor the sinking of their efforts below what could be done in faith, but the exaggeration of their thinking toward impossible wishes and the inflammation of their will toward endeavors beyond their strength. Faith protects against this because it liberates from selfish striving after perfection and greatness, desires the divine will, and obeys God's leadership. If they act in faith, they purify themselves from their pretensions and proud independence, and they endeavor to utilize what they have been apportioned in their inner life and in their

---

[1] Schlatter isn't talking about the roles of men and women in using the word *egalitarian*. He refers to the desire to supplant hierarchy and make all people equal in terms of gifts, responsibilities, and authority.

association with the others. This dispels fantasies and opens the eye to reality.[2]

Paul's instructions here are immensely practical. We must recognize what God made us to be and avoid trying to become what we are not. It is tempting to attempt to imitate others and to live based on the faith that God has given them. As we consider someone we admire or who has influenced us, we may start to think that we should become what they are. We need to consider, however, what God has called us to be. If God hasn't called us to be a missionary, we should not try to become a missionary. I have seen some students come to seminary to study because they have had a profound encounter with God, and they conclude that they are called to the ministry. Now they may be called to the ministry, but some of them clearly were not meant for certain ministry positions, and they feel disappointed and perhaps even disillusioned when they don't get a particular ministry position. We should recognize, further, that joy in the Lord doesn't necessarily mean you should be in ministry. We need enthusiastic believers

> *We need enthusiastic believers in law offices, banks, service industries, and as plumbers, electricians, and builders.*

---

[2] Adolf Schlatter, *Romans: The Righteousness of God*, translated by S. S. Schatzmann (Peabody, MA: Hendrickson, 1995), 231.

in law offices, banks, service industries, and as plumbers, electricians, and builders.

The Lord calls upon us to assess our gifts realistically, and here is where other people can help us, for our gifts don't just reflect what we think about ourselves. Other members of the body of Christ can and must help us discern and confirm the gifts in our lives. Sometimes they help us see that the gift we thought we had isn't the area we should concentrate our energies after all. The need to discern our calling is immensely practical and applies in so many areas of life. You may not be gifted musically, or an eloquent speaker, but you notice those in pain and reach out to them (mercy!), or willingly serve behind the scenes (helps!). We are to bloom where God has planted us and find the niche where God has placed us, and then live with all our strength for God's glory.

A realistic assessment of our lives and our talents and gifts brings great contentment about our place in life if we rest in God. How many live in unhappiness because they aren't content with what God has given them? They long and grasp for a greatness God didn't intend for them to have. I had a young student say to me once that he was going to be the next Francis Schaeffer! He was young, and I am sure he soon realized that such a desire was a fantasy and a dream out of accord with reality. We are not to long for a greatness God doesn't intend for us to have. We are to think in a sensible way about ourselves and should not think too highly about ourselves. We are to be like John the Baptist who was content that Jesus was increasing and he was decreasing (John 3:30). John's desire to decrease is remarkable because his disciples were egging him on, worried about his reputation (John 3:26). John recognized, however, that his place in life was appointed by God, that "no one can receive anything unless it has been given to him from heaven" (John 3:27). We should not long, then, for greatness that God doesn't intend us to have, but should find contentment in our lives by not overestimating our gifts or wishing for gifts that have not been given to us.

The Diversity and Results of Gifts Are from God

Third, the variety of spiritual gifts and the results of those gifts come from God himself. What we see here is similar to the admonition in Romans 12:3, where Paul speaks against the desire for equality, the desire for everyone to be the same. Such a desire goes against one of God's fundamental purposes in giving the gifts. "Now there are different gifts, but the same Spirit. There are different ministries, but the same Lord. And there are different activities, but the same God produces each gift in each person" (1 Cor. 12:4–6). In these wonderful Trinitarian verses, we see that we must avoid the mistake of thinking that God wants us all to have the same gifts, the same ministries, and the same results. It is striking how the Spirit, the Son, and the Father are included in these verses, which impresses upon us the divine origin of the gifts. We see here that all the members of the Trinity work together in granting us gifts. Our gifts come from the Father, the Son, and the Spirit, showing that the source of our gifts is the Triune God.

Paul never thought that each person in the church would have the same gift, nor does he think they should have the same gift. "Now you are the body of Christ, and individual members of it. And God has appointed these in the church: first apostles, second prophets, third teachers, next miracles, then gifts of healing, helping, administrating, various kinds of tongues. Are all apostles? Are all prophets? Are all teachers? Do all do miracles? Do all have gifts of healing? Do all speak in other tongues? Do all interpret? But desire the greater gifts" (1 Cor. 12:27–31). Paul's words here could hardly be clearer. It was never God's intention that a person possess or exercise all the gifts; he wants to remove from their minds any conception that all the gifts are equally accessible to all believers.

Our Gifts Don't Make Us Inferior or Superior

Fourth, having a different spiritual gift doesn't mean we are inferior or superior. How we feel about our gifts is a central part of what Paul teaches, and so he teaches in more detail the implications of the unity and diversity of the body of Christ. In 1 Corinthians 12:14 he says, "Even so the body is not made up of one part but of many" (NIV). The body of Christ is characterized by unity and diversity. We are one body in Christ, and yet at the same time the body consists of many different members.

Some members of the body are tempted at various times to feel inferior. "If the foot should say, 'Because I am not a hand, I do not belong to the body,' it would not for that reason stop being part of the body" (1 Cor. 12:15). *You may think, I am only a lowly and clumsy foot and not a useful and productive hand.* Conversely, you may think that you are only an ugly and misshapen ear instead of a beautiful eye. "And if the ear should say, 'Because I am not an eye, I do not belong to the body,' it would not for that reason stop being part of the body" (1 Cor. 12:16).

> *Having a different spiritual gift doesn't mean we are inferior or superior.*

The body of Christ is composed of many members. There is not a boring kind of sameness. It is tempting for us to compare ourselves with others and to feel inferior. We constantly wonder whether we stack up, whether we are living up to the standards of others. In doing so, we lose God's perspective of the body and of our ministry. A foot may think, *I am not as attractive and valuable as a hand,* and thus think it has no vital role to play in the body, but nevertheless it is a vital and crucial part of the body. Without our feet or with an injured foot, we are severely handicapped. Similarly, an ear may not be as attractive as an eye, but it is vital to the body. If our ears start giving us problems, we quickly notice.

We sometimes mistake our feelings of inferiority for humility, but feelings of inferiority are a kind of inverted pride. We don't want others to see our deficiencies. Still, it is instructive that Paul doesn't rebuke the inferior-feeling Corinthians for pride but encourages them. We ought not to think that pride should always be reproved or exposed. Often when we feel weak we need encouragement. Paul reminds us that we are made in God's image, that we all play a valuable role. We don't simply say to a person suffering from feelings of uselessness: "You are proud and arrogant too!" Instead, Paul sets an example that we should remind them of their important role in the body. He encourages their hearts.

If you think, *I don't have any gifts. I am of no value to anyone,* your thinking about yourself is off-center. God has given you faith, and he created and made you to be a significant help to others. Don't reject what God has done in your life by putting yourself down. We may feel that our gifts are insignificant or unimportant, but we are mistaken. The contribution of every member of the body matters. What you contribute to your church is crucial, and that is true of every member of the body. If you are

> *The contribution of every member of the body matters.*

feeling inferior about your role in the body, then your feelings, as are our feelings so often, are off-track.

While no member of the body is inferior, we also see that no member of the body is comprehensive. We see this clearly in 1 Corinthians 12:17–20. "If the whole body were an eye, where would the hearing be? If the whole body were an ear, where would the sense of smell be? But as it is, God has arranged each one of the parts in the body just as he wanted. And if they were all the same part, where would the body be? As it is, there are many parts, but one body." Imagine if your body was only an eye, and a huge eye rolled into the room instead of your entire body. Or imagine that instead of a human body as a whole, we were all massive ears. Wouldn't that be grotesque in the extreme? Paul reminds us of elementary but crucial truths here. Eyes without ears are not complete bodies. Ears without noses are not complete bodies. No member of the body is comprehensive; bodies by definition are made up of many members, and they don't function as bodies otherwise.

As I write this, the World Series is going on. Last night, Clayton Kershaw, of the Los Angeles Dodgers, pitched a masterpiece, and the Dodgers beat the Houston Astros in Game One of the Series 3–1.[3] But try to imagine Kershaw, as great as he is, saying that he didn't need the rest of his team to win. He could not win the game all by himself since baseball is a

---

[3] The Astros, however, ended up winning the World Series!

team game. A pitcher needs a catcher, and a second baseman, and every other player on the field. And even if a pitcher were a great hitter (and Kershaw is quite good as pitchers go!), he couldn't win the game without other hitters. No business or team works effectively if someone tries to do all the jobs him or herself; teamwork is necessary in every part of life.

Notice also what the verse doesn't say. It doesn't say that we belong to one another if we *feel* especially close to one another. Our belonging to one another isn't based on our feelings or on friendships. Our head and hands aren't united because they feel especially close to one another. Our unity as a body is a fact, whether we feel it or not, whether we naturally like each other or not. The wonderful thing about the church is that God has called us together with all our differences. We are called upon to love one another, even if we wouldn't naturally like one another. The church isn't a club where people of the same interest or same personalities gather together. The church consists of those who are called together by God's grace to be the body of Christ: rich and poor, black and white, male and female, and white-collar and blue-collar workers. The elbow and the ear may not seem to have anything in common, but they are both a part of the body. In the same way, church members who are very different still have the most

> *Our belonging to one another isn't based on our feelings or on friendships.*

important thing in common, because we are all connected to the same body.

We also see here that no member of the body is superior. Paul circles back to what we saw in Romans 12:3 but hits it from another angle. "The eye cannot say to the hand, 'I don't need you!' Or again, the head can't say to the feet, 'I don't need you!' On the contrary, those parts of the body that are weaker are indispensable. And those parts of the body that we consider less honorable, we clothe these with greater honor, and our unrespectable parts are treated with greater respect, which our respectable parts do not need" (1 Cor. 12:21–24). Here Paul tackles arrogance, the feeling that we are the indispensable part of the body. The eye may be beautiful and begin to think other parts of the body are unnecessary, and a head may begin to think that the feet are useless. Such pride is irrational and self-destructive. Even if we don't realize it, we desperately need every part of the body. The parts of the body we don't show to the world are still necessary for the body to function.

As I write, I am reading a biography of Peter the Great of Russia, who had magnificent ideas as the Czar of Russia about how Russia could progress. But the ideas in his head weren't always easy to implement since he needed help from his citizens to make them a reality. So too, if any member of the body thinks he or she can dispense with weaker members, they will soon find out they are radically mistaken. Those parts of the body that seem to be weaker and less necessary are crucial to the smooth running of the body. Every member is needed to carry out what the body needs to do, and no member should think he or she is more important. Pride introduces serious weakness into the body, and such conceit in ourselves should be identified and put to death daily.

The Gifts Are Sovereignly Given

Fifth, our gifts are not to be ascribed to our own spirituality but to the sovereignty of the Spirit. As human beings we are wired (because of original sin) to take credit for our accomplishments. We know that the Scripture says everything we have is a gift, that we have accomplished nothing on our own (1 Cor. 4:7). Still, we are curved in upon ourselves and begin to congratulate ourselves for the gifts we have or the effects of our ministry. Or, conversely, we might lament that we don't have the gift we should have or believe we deserve. We may fall into discouragement and even depression over who and what we are.

Paul reminds us of God's sovereignty, teaching us that the gift we have is a result of God's will, not ours. We see this in 1 Corinthians 12:7–11. "A manifestation of the Spirit is given to each person for the common good: to one is given a message of wisdom through the Spirit, to another, a message of knowledge by the same Spirit, to another, faith by the same Spirit, to another, gifts of healing by the one Spirit, to another, the performing of miracles, to another, prophecy, to another, distinguishing between spirits, to another, different kinds of tongues, to another, interpretation of tongues. One and the same Spirit is active in all these, distributing to each person as he wills." Paul hammers home in these verses that the various gifts all derive from the Holy Spirit. They are *gifts* after all!

We can rest in and rejoice over the gifts God has given us because the Spirit has given them to us "as he wills" (1 Cor. 12:11). Incidentally, this is an important verse on the personality and personhood of the Holy Spirit, since only a person can choose or will something. We see the same emphasis on God's sovereignty and appointment of our gifts elsewhere in chapter 12. We read in 1 Corinthians 12:18, "But as it is, God has arranged each one of the parts in the body just as he wanted." And in 1 Corinthians 12:28 Paul lists various gifts and gifted persons, and says, "God has appointed these in the church." Incidentally, we have a good example here of Father and the Son doing the same work, which points us to the doctrine of the Trinity. Paul emphasizes that the Spirit gives us gifts, but he also says that the Father determines our gifts. Your gift doesn't reflect what *you* have accomplished. It signifies what God has for his own wise purposes given to you for the sake of the church. Let's give praise and give thanks to God for the gifts he has given to us, and let's entrust our lives to him, knowing that he will fulfill the purpose intended when he created us. As Psalm 138:8 says, "The LORD will fulfill his purpose for me."

We don't have to fret and worry that our lives have been spent in vain if we are endeavoring to please the Lord. He has given us the gifts and the ministry he intended for us to have, and he is working out his will in the world and in our lives as well.

Conclusion

Five truths about spiritual gifts have been set forth in this chapter. First, all gifts are to be exercised under Christ's lordship. Gifts aren't designed for our own happiness (though they do bring us joy!) but to serve our Lord Jesus Christ. Second, we are to think reasonably about our gifts. We are prone to overestimate the importance of our gifts and to exalt ourselves instead of humbling ourselves. Third, the gifts given by God are remarkably diverse, and such diversity is to be celebrated. We recognize that God doesn't want everyone to be the same or to function in the same way. Fourth, our gifts don't make us inferior or superior to others. The gifts don't reflect our spiritual strength but are given to strengthen the church. Fifth, we must remember that our gifts are sovereignly appointed by the Holy Spirit, by God himself. The gifts we have reflect God's grace and goodness in our lives, and we can't take credit for the gifts we have or worry about gifts we don't possess. God has wisely given us the gifts we have for the sake of the church and for the sake of his great name.

Discussion Questions

1. What does it mean that the lordship of Christ is the criterion by which gifts are assessed (p. 30)? Why does this matter?

2. Why is it so important to be who God has called you to be, rather then trying to imitate the gifts of others?

3. Have you ever seen a church attach inferiority or superiority to people with particular spiritual gifts? How can we prevent this from happening?

4. Why should we remember God's sovereignty over the gifts?

Chapter Four

Five More Truths about Spiritual Gifts

Gifts Given to Edify the Church

We continue to consider practical pastoral truths in this chapter and turn toward five more truths which are important for our lives. First, we need to consider the purpose of the gifts.

God has given us gifts to build up the body (Eph. 4:12–16), to bring unity to the church (1 Cor. 12:25–26), and to edify the church (cf. also 1 Cor. 14:1–40). We cannot do a full exegesis of the relevant texts here and will reserve 1 Corinthians 14:1–40 for later discussion, but we will look briefly at two texts to establish the point. We read in Ephesians 4:11–16,

And he himself gave some to be apostles, some prophets, some evangelists, some pastors and teachers, equipping the saints for the work of ministry, to build up the body of Christ, until we all reach unity in the faith and in the knowledge of God's Son, growing into maturity with a stature measured by Christ's fullness. Then we will no longer be little children, tossed by the waves and blown around by every wind of teaching, by human cunning with cleverness in the techniques of deceit. But speaking the truth in love, let us grow in every way into him who is the head Christ. From him the whole body, fitted and knit together by every supporting ligament, promotes the growth of the body for building up itself in love by the proper working of each individual part.

Paul speaks of gifted persons here rather than gifts, but it is also the case that people are called prophets because they have the gift of prophecy, and people are called teachers because they have the gift of teaching. We recognize that Paul refers to gifted persons, but it is also legitimate to speak of the gifts themselves from this text.

Gifts were given to equip believers for ministry. We see in verse 16 that "every supporting ligament" and "each individual part" plays a role. The purpose of the gifts is "to build up the body of Christ" (Eph. 4:12). The building up of the body leads to its unity and its stability and maturity. Such maturity means that the church becomes more like Jesus Christ, and at the same time the church will have a doctrinal solidity. Immature churches are also poorly taught churches. Thus, they are doctrinally unstable, blown here and there by false teachings. We see here that the maturity of the church is both behavioral and doctrinal. The church represents the character of Christ and the thinking of Christ so that it is both godly and vigilant for the truth of the gospel.

We also see from Ephesians that the gifts were not given so that we would marvel over our abilities or covet the abilities of others. Nor were they given so that we would experience satisfaction and fulfillment in our lives. Still further, the gifts weren't given so that we could realize our self-potential. The gifts were given so that we would equip and strengthen other believers, and thus the gifts are others-centered, not self-centered.

A central text on spiritual gifts is 1 Corinthians 12:24–26. "Instead, God has put the body together, giving greater honor to the less honorable, so that there would be no division in the body, but that the members would have the same concern for each other. So if one member suffers, all the members suffer with it; if one member is honored, all the members rejoice with it." This text is quite remarkable. God gave us gifts so that we would not be divided but united. As we exercise our gifts, we demonstrate that we care about what is happening in one another's lives, that we truly love one another. What this means is expressed in a very practical way. If one of the members of the church is hurting, we grieve with them. And if one of our members is rejoicing, we rejoice with them. The gifts are cruciform, for as we exercise the gifts, we give ourselves for the sake of others, just as Christ did on the cross.

> *The gifts are cruciform, for as we exercise the gifts, we give ourselves for the sake of others, just as Christ did on the cross.*

When pastors prepare sermons, they express their love for the flock. The person who works on the sound in the building does so to show love to the flock. When we meet with others and encourage them or admonish them, we show our love for them. None of us can do alone what the body of Christ can do together. We need the whole body to show this kind of concern for others. This isn't just the task of elders or of pastors, but the ministry description for each one of us. The needs are too great to be met simply by one small group of people.

If our churches show this kind of love and concern for one another, they will be built up and mature. At the same time, we will have an influence on unbelievers. People are hungry for this kind of love, for this kind of caring. We ought not to be thinking when we join together as a congregation, *Are people here loving me this way? Are my needs being met?* We should be thinking instead, *Am I loving people like that? Am I reaching out to the hurting? Am I rejoicing with those who rejoice?* Spiritual gifts are exercised when we sacrifice ourselves for the sake of others, when we love others for Christ's sake.

The Baptism of the Spirit at Conversion

Second, the baptism of the Spirit takes place at conversion. The central text for our purposes is 1 Corinthians 12:13. "For by one Spirit we were all baptized into one body—whether Jews or Greeks, whether slaves or free—and we were all given one Spirit to drink." Pentecostals and some charismatics have often argued that the baptism of the Spirit occurs after conversion, and that it involves a special empowering for service. In a few cases, they have even argued that it is a mark of spiritual maturity. Even Martin Lloyd Jones, the great twentieth-century preacher, maintained that not all believers were baptized with the Spirit, and he saw the baptism of the Spirit as an experience for only some. Thus, he believed the baptism of the Spirit was a post-conversion reality.

Paul's words about the baptism of the Spirit bring to mind other texts in the New Testament that refer to the same theme.[1] Five texts, apart from 1 Corinthians 12:13, refer to the baptism

---

[1] We should note up front that the phrase "baptism of the Spirit" is never used in the New Testament. In the New Testament, we always find a verbal form, though I will continue to use the nominal form.

of the Spirit (Matt. 3:11; Mark 1:8; Luke 3:16; Acts 1:5; and 11:16). It is striking that all five of these texts contain prophecy about Jesus baptizing his followers with the Holy Spirit. In other words, these five texts are in a sense just one text, for they are either Gospel parallels or they restate the promise that Jesus would baptize with the Spirit. So once we quote one of these verses, we have quoted them all, for they all say essentially the same thing.

To put it another way, there are actually only two distinct texts that speak of the baptism of the Spirit in the New Testament. The first is the baptism of the Spirit predicted by John the Baptist and fulfilled on the day of Pentecost and in Cornelius and his friends, and the New Testament refers to this saying five times. The second and only other text that speaks of the baptism of the Spirit is found here in 1 Corinthians 12:13.

We need to consider briefly John the Baptist's words, which we find in Matthew 3:11, "I baptize you with water for repentance, but the one who is coming after me is more powerful than I. I am not worthy to remove his sandals. He himself will baptize you with the Holy Spirit and fire." We see here that John the Baptist and Jesus Christ are the baptizers, but they use different elements. John baptizes with water, and Jesus baptizes with the Holy Spirit. We have already seen that the promise that Jesus would baptize with the Spirit is fulfilled on the day of Pentecost (Acts 1:5; 11:16). The great promises in the Old Testament are fulfilled in the baptism of the Spirit, for the Old Testament prophets looked forward to the day when the Spirit would be poured out, and the promises of a new creation, a new covenant, and a new exodus would be realized (cf. Isa. 32:15; 44:3; Ezek. 36:26–27; 37:14; 39:29; Joel 2:28–29). Certainly this promise was fulfilled among all believers in Jesus Christ on the Day of Pentecost. If anyone wasn't baptized with the Spirit on that day, they didn't belong to Jesus Christ; they were not truly a believer.

We find something similar in Acts 10:44–48 where Cornelius and his friends receive the Spirit. Certainly what happened to Cornelius and his friends can be described as the baptism of the Spirit (Acts 11:16), but there is no suggestion that some of those gathered weren't baptized by the Spirit on this occasion. Actually, those who had received the Spirit and who were baptized with the Spirit were also baptized with water (Acts 10:47). We see a close association between baptism in water and baptism with the Spirit. This is not an argument for baptismal regeneration; the point is that baptism with the Spirit and baptism with water were both *initiatory events*. The fact that Cornelius and his friends were baptized with the Spirit meant they were qualified to be baptized with water! There is no hint that some who were baptized with water (i.e., those who gave every evidence of being believers) were somehow not baptized with the Spirit.

Some bring up the experience of the Samaritans in Acts at this point. Actually, the phrase "baptism of the Spirit" isn't used of the Samaritans. Even if one were to argue for a connection theologically, the Samaritan experience can hardly be used as a paradigm today. The Samaritans believed in the gospel preached by Philip the evangelist, and yet when they believed they did not receive the Holy Spirit (Acts 8:4–24). Such a state of affairs is exceedingly strange, since it is unheard of that one could believe in Jesus Christ and not receive the Spirit! We notice that the language used is "receiving the Spirit" (Acts 8:15), not "baptism of the Spirit."

If one doesn't have the Holy Spirit, then one isn't a believer, as Paul makes very clear in Romans 8:9. "You, however, are not in the flesh, but in the Spirit, if indeed the Spirit of God lives in you. If anyone does not have the Spirit of Christ, he does not belong to him." We know from Galatians 3:1–5 and Acts 15:7–11 that the indisputable evidence that one is a believer is the reception of the Holy Spirit. Paul assures the Galatians that they don't need to be circumcised to become believers, and as proof he reminds them that they received the Holy Spirit by faith and not because they kept the works of the law (Gal. 3:2, 5). Peter makes the same point at the Apostolic Council in Acts 15. The newly converted Gentiles don't need to receive circumcision for salvation because God has granted the Spirit to Gentiles apart from the observance of the law. Since they have received the Spirit, they are clearly Christians!

But this brings us back again to the strange world of the Samaritans in Acts 8. How is it that they had placed their faith in Jesus Christ and yet hadn't received the Spirit? Such a thing is unheard of! Furthermore, why wasn't the gift of the Spirit given to the Samaritans through the agency of Philip the Evangelist? The Philip in view here isn't Philip the apostle, for all the apostles remained in Jerusalem (Acts 8:3). No, this is Philip one of the seven appointed to take care of the Hellenistic widows (Acts 6:5). Philip could not give the Spirit, and instead Peter and John had to come down from Jerusalem and lay hands on the Samaritans so that they received the Spirit (Acts 8:14–17).

The point of the story isn't that there is a normative pattern where the hands of the apostles have to be laid on someone to receive the Spirit. We know this because Cornelius and his friends received the Spirit without anyone laying hands on them (Acts 10:44–48). We must recognize that what happened to the Samaritans was a unique occurrence in redemptive history. No one believes in Jesus Christ and doesn't receive the Spirit. There is no other example of this.

So how do we explain what is going on? The best answer is that the Spirit wasn't given immediately to the Samaritans because of the cultural breach between the Jews and the Samaritans. The division between Jews and Samaritans shows up several times in the New Testament, and perhaps reaches back to the exile of the northern kingdom to Assyria (722 BC) and perhaps even further back in history. We see indications in Ezra 4 and Nehemiah 4 of tensions between Jews in Jerusalem and the Samaritans. The Samaritans believed only the Pentateuch was authoritative, and they built a rival temple on Mount Gerizim perhaps in the fifth century BC. The Hasmonean king John Hyrcanus burned down the temple on Mount Gerizim some time around 110 BC, which further inflamed hatred between Jews and Samaritans.

The divide between Jews and Samaritans shows up often in the New Testament. The Twelve are commissioned to preach to "the lost sheep of the house of Israel" and to avoid the Samaritans (Matt. 10:5–6). We see here that the Samaritans aren't considered to be part of Israel. Along the same lines, the Samaritans didn't welcome Jesus and his disciples as he contemplated a journey through their territory (Luke 9:52–56). The disciples wanted to summon fire from heaven to destroy the Samaritans, but Jesus rebuked them. In the famous parable of the Good Samaritan, the actions of the Samaritan stand out precisely because he wasn't part of Israel (Luke 10:25–37). So too, it was astonishing that the only leper whom Jesus healed that returned and gave thanks was a Samaritan (Luke 17:11–19). Jesus' conversation with the Samaritan woman (John 4:4–42) was surprising at many levels, particularly because "Jews do not associate with Samaritans" (John 4:9).

Here we find an explanation, then, for why the Spirit wasn't poured out when the Samaritans believed in Jesus, but when the apostles Peter and John laid hands on them. The purpose for the delay in granting the Spirit was the Lord's desire to end the cultural and theological breach between Jews and

Samaritans. The Samaritans could not and must not start their own Christian movement apart from the church in Jerusalem. In the union of Jews and Samaritans in the church of Jesus Christ we see a fulfillment of Ezekiel 37, which prophesied the reunion of the northern and southern kingdom. This reintegration of the Samaritans in the people of God placed the Samaritans firmly under the authority of the apostles in Jerusalem.

The temporal interval in the Samaritan experience between believing in Jesus and receiving the Spirit was a unique event in redemptive history, purposed by God to reveal the tearing down of the wall between Jews and Samaritans. It has never happened since, and it will never happen again. There is no basis in the story for concluding that the baptism of the Spirit is subsequent to conversion.

Another text that is sometimes suggested as pointing to subsequence with reference to baptism of the Spirit is the story of the twelve disciples of Ephesus in Acts 19. In truth, however, this story doesn't support such a reading. The Ephesian twelve were baptized only into the baptism introduced by John the Baptist (Acts 19:3). They were living in a redemptive historical time warp, for they had not yet heard that the promised Holy Spirit had been poured out (Acts 19:2). When Paul preached to them, they *believed* in Jesus and were baptized in his name (Acts 19:4–5). Upon believing in Jesus, the Spirit came upon them and they spoke in tongues and prophesied (Acts 19:6).

The story doesn't indicate that the baptism of the Spirit is subsequent to conversion because the Ephesian twelve received the Spirit immediately upon believing in Jesus and being baptized in his name.

We have seen in Acts that there is no basis for saying that the baptism of the Spirit is subsequent to conversion, and the same conclusion should be drawn from 1 Corinthians 12:13. I suggest that 1 Corinthians 12:13 should be translated in a way that accords with Matthew 3:11 and its parallels. The verb "baptize" is actually passive, and so should be translated like this, "we were all baptized with or in the Holy Spirit by Jesus Christ." The NASB translates the verse to say we were baptized "by" the Holy Spirit, but the passive verb suggests that Jesus Christ is the baptizer and the Spirit is the person in which one is plunged at baptism. It is unlikely that baptism in the Spirit means something different in the Gospels from what we find in Paul. More specifically, Luke and Paul traveled together, and it seems probable that their understanding of baptism of the Spirit, which was clearly an important theme in Luke, would match.

What is crystal clear in 1 Corinthians 12:13 is that baptism with the Spirit occurs at conversion, and that it cannot be a second experience after conversion. Paul emphasizes in the verse that *all* Christians were baptized with the Spirit, not just some, whereas in second experience theology, only some have received the gift subsequent to conversion. Indeed, Paul is particularly emphatic about the gift being given to all, for he specifies that *all* have been baptized with the Spirit, demonstrated in his words, "whether Jews or Greeks, whether slaves or free." Paul then adds the word *all* again, saying, "we were all given one Spirit to drink" (12:13).

We should note again that the word *baptized* itself suggests that this experience took place at conversion. For in Paul's mind, the baptism with the Spirit is inevitably linked with baptism in water. Remember, in Paul's day, virtually all Christians were baptized almost immediately after their conversion, and so the very language of baptism suggests an initiation experience, the beginning of the Christian life. Some Pentecostals have conceded that the first part of 1 Corinthians 12:13 relates to conversion, but understand the second part of the verse to be a second blessing of the Spirit after conversion, where Paul says, "We were all given one Spirit to drink." But this reading is very unlikely. The two statements in the verse are parallel. At conversion, Jesus Christ plunged believers into the Holy Spirit, so that we are immersed with the Spirit when we are saved. In the same way, at our conversion, we are made to drink of the Spirit, and we live because we drink from the water of life. The one we are immersed into is the one we drink from.

Imagine that you are plunged down into a pool of water, and this water is also the best water in the world to drink. It is the water of life to you. That is what happens Paul says when you were saved. You were plunged down into the Spirit and you drank him in. Paul's main point here is this: when we are baptized or plunged into the Spirit and made to drink of the Spirit, we become part of Christ's body, the church. We share a common bond in the body of Christ because every one of us has drunk deeply of the Holy Spirit and been plunged into the Spirit. To read Paul to say that some Christians do not share this experience is to misconstrue his words and say that some Christians are not part of the church. But this is impossible, for if anyone is not part of the church of Jesus Christ, he or she is unsaved.

> *When we are baptized or plunged into the Spirit and made to drink of the Spirit, we become part of Christ's body, the church.*

Edification through Understanding

Third, edification comes especially through the mind, through understandable teaching. The emphasis on understanding is obvious in 1 Corinthians 14:1–19, for Paul labors to say that believers are built up when they grasp and perceive what is going on. The passage is long, but we should read all of 1 Corinthians 14:1–19:

> Pursue love and desire spiritual gifts, and especially that you may prophesy. For the person who speaks in another tongue is not speaking to people but to God, since no one understands him; he speaks mysteries in

the Spirit. On the other hand, the person who prophesies speaks to people for their strengthening, encouragement, and consolation. The person who speaks in another tongue builds himself up, but the one who prophesies builds up the church. I wish all of you spoke in other tongues, but even more that you prophesied. The person who prophesies is greater than the person who speaks in tongues, unless he interprets so that the church may be built up.

So now, brothers and sisters, if I come to you speaking in other tongues, how will I benefit you unless I speak to you with a revelation or knowledge or prophecy or teaching? Even lifeless instruments that produce sounds—whether flute or harp if they don't make a distinction in the notes, how will what is played on the flute or harp be recognized? In fact, if the bugle makes an unclear sound, who will prepare for battle? In the same way, unless you use your tongue for intelligible speech, how will what is spoken be known? For you will be speaking into the air. There are doubtless many different kinds of languages in the world, none is without meaning. Therefore, if I do not know the meaning of the language, I will be a foreigner to the speaker, and the speaker will be a foreigner to me.

So also you—since you are zealous for spiritual gifts, seek to excel in building up the church. Therefore the person who speaks in another tongue should pray that he can interpret. For if I pray in another tongue, my spirit prays, but my understanding is unfruitful. What then? I will pray with the spirit, and I will also pray with my understanding. I will sing praise with the spirit, and I will also sing praise with my understanding. Otherwise, if you praise with the spirit, how will the outsider say "Amen" at your giving of thanks, since he does not know what you are saying? For you may very well be giving thanks, but the other person is not being built up. I thank God that I speak in other tongues more than all of you; yet in the church I would rather speak five words with my understanding, in order to teach others also, than ten thousand words in another tongue.

We could attend to many features in these verses, and some of them we will return to later. Here we want to see that Paul centers on understanding, on comprehending what is said. A few observations on the text will impress upon us the importance of comprehension.

Paul uses illustrations so that the Corinthians will see the importance of cognition. Paul tells us that if someone plays a flute or harp, but there isn't a distinct melody—only senseless anarchy—then people won't recognize it as music (14:7). They won't even know that a flute or harp is being played. In the same way, if a bugler doesn't blow his trumpet forcefully and clearly, it will not be evident that he is sounding the alarm for war (14:8). Paul thinks tongue-speaking without interpretation is useless to people. It is like speaking into the air (14:9). It is all sound and fury signifying nothing. We are only edified or strengthened if we understand what is being said.

Paul uses an illustration from unknown languages in 14:10–11. All languages have structure and meaning, but if we don't understand the language, we are not helped when we are with people who speak in that language. The words may have tremendous significance, even for our own lives, but since we don't understand what they are saying, we are clueless. Those who have traveled in another country and don't know the language of the residents know exactly what I am saying. We are left on the outside.

I worked in my father's plant nursery with Spanish-speakers for many years. Often, they seemed to be having a great time laughing and talking. It all seemed very interesting, but I had no idea what they were talking about! I was on the outside, since I didn't know Spanish.

Paul draws the application for his readers in 14:12, "So also you—since you are zealous for spiritual gifts, seek to excel in building up the church." The *way* the church is edified is through *understandable* words. So, the one who speaks in a tongue should also pray that he may interpret what is said.

For edification, as verse 14 says, comes when the mind is fruitfully involved in what is being said. We see the emphasis on the mind in verse 15 as well, "What then? I will pray with the spirit, and I will also pray with my understanding. I will sing praise with the spirit, and I will also sing praise with my understanding." The crucial role of understanding is made clear in verse 16, "Otherwise, if you praise with the spirit, how will the outsider say 'Amen' at your giving of thanks, since he does not know what you are saying?" Edification comes when we comprehend what another is saying, when we understand it. It would be utterly misleading to say "amen" if we don't understand and agree with what is being said.

If you have ever spoken with a person whom it was difficult to understand, you understand well what is being said here. Sadly, my aunt had radical mouth surgery. She would occasionally call me on the phone, and it was extremely difficult for me to discern what she was trying to articulate as she talked. At the same time, it was awkward to constantly ask her to repeat her statements. When my aunt and I didn't understand each other, our conversations weren't helpful or edifying.

Paul is thankful (14:18) that he speaks in tongues more than them all, but in church he wants to engage the mind, so that others may be instructed and learn (14:19), for that is much better than speaking ten thousand words in a tongue which people do not comprehend. The main point in 14:6–19 is easy to grasp because Paul repeats it again and again. Understanding and edification come through the mind.

Protestants have always believed in education and the importance of reading, because we believe that people are strengthened in their relationship with God as they gain understanding. This idea is implicitly communicated in Ephesians 3:4, where Paul says, "By reading this you are able to understand my insight into the mystery of Christ." Paul connects understanding with the ability to read and understand.

The greatest reason for education is the opportunity to read and understand God's Word. God could have used a number of means to strengthen us. He could have just zapped us when we became Christians, and in that way we would be instantly transformed. God could have us go into a little room with an energy field, and then *shazaam!* we come out spiritual. But he desires us to grow in our relationship to him slowly, as we gain more understanding. Some might think that we would become more like God as we sit in a posture of meditation and chant a mantra again and again like "Saki Um," but this text tells us that this is not the way to spiritual growth, for the mind is uninvolved. Others might think something ecstatic like speaking in tongues is the key to spiritual life, but Paul exalts understanding over stunning experiences. Our relationship with God is predicated on understanding him.

Mark Dever, pastor of Capitol Hill Baptist Church, points out that we may feel we have a good relationship with our dog, but if we came home from church, and our dog talked with us, the relationship would change dramatically because we would now have a dialogical relationship with our dog. We would not only tell our dog what to do; presumably our dog would sometimes tell us what to do! The primary pathway to spiritual growth is not even prayer, as important as prayer is. Prayer feeds off the Word of God, the understanding that comes from the Scriptures. Without that, our prayers will be remarkably off center. The famous verses in Romans 12:1–2 warn us against being conformed to this world. How can we resist the pressures of this world? By being transformed by the renewal of our minds!

Concentrate on Your Gift

Fourth, we are also instructed to concentrate on our gifts. We read in Romans 12:6–8, "According to the grace given to us, we have different gifts: If prophecy, use it according to the proportion of one's faith; if service, use it in service; if teaching, in teaching; if exhorting, in exhortation; giving, with generosity; leading, with diligence; showing mercy, with cheerfulness." We see here that gifts are a sign of God's grace and love in our lives, and the various gifts testify to the diversity of the body of Christ. As believers, we are not all the same, and the differences among us are due to God's grace.

A couple of observations should be made about this text. In verses 7–8 Paul lists three gifts and says that believers should concentrate on the gift one has. For instance, those who have a gift of service should concentrate on serving. Those with a gift of teaching should center their ministry on their teaching, while those who have a gift of exhortation and encouragement should devote themselves to encouraging others.

What Paul says here applies to all the gifts and is immensely practical. We should pour our energy into the gifts we have. Of course, we must be careful and avoid an overreaction. We must not say, "I won't serve because I have the gift of teaching," or, "I don't do evangelism because I don't have the gift of sharing the gospel with others." On the other hand, life is short, and God has designed the body so that it functions best when we concentrate on the gifts we have. We are to spend our time maximizing the particular gift God has given us. To do such is not unspiritual or selfish but wise.

I remember a student coming to me, telling me that he was so discouraged because he was spending all his time studying Greek and Hebrew, and yet he was doing terrible in the classes. How could he be a great language student like he was supposed to be? All of us, of course, have to work hard and be disciplined in areas we are not skilled in, but I told him, "If you are trying so hard and not doing well, God doesn't want you to concentrate on languages. That isn't your gift. God has gifted you in other matters and you should concentrate on those." He was visibly relieved and encouraged in hearing this. And it fits with what Paul says here. Don't ignore areas where you are weak, but focus your energy on where you are strong and rejoice in the gifts God has given you. We may waste time trying to become experts in an arena where we are not gifted, and usually such endeavors are due to false expectations we have put on ourselves or the false expectations others have imposed upon us. Give yourself completely and joyfully to the work God has given you to do.

Paul also gives three specific exhortations in these verses, reminding us about our responsibilities in exercising the gifts God has given us. First, those who give money should do so generously. We read in 2 Corinthians 9:7 that "God loves a cheerful giver." If you have a gift of giving, beware of a stingy and crabby spirit taking hold of you. Ask God to give you a spirit of lavishness and delight so that giving is not motivated by the praise of people but is for the glory of God. We have a great promise in Philippians 4:19: "My God shall supply all your needs according to his riches in glory in Christ Jesus." We exercise the gift of giving the way God intends when we give gladly. The Macedonians mentioned in 2 Corinthians 8 were poor, but giving wasn't an onerous burden for them. They didn't give with a sigh, as if giving was a necessary but painful duty. Rather, they found great joy in giving, even begging Paul for the privilege of giving.

Second, those who lead are to do so with zeal and diligence. Leaders have a great responsibility. Leaders should be accountable to others, and clear lines of accountability should be established. Still, many leaders aren't truly accountable to others since those under their authority fear or hesitate to speak to someone over them. After all, some leaders have been known to fire those under them who point out their deficiencies.

Leaders may become accustomed to doing what they wish to do with their time, and they often enjoy great freedom in their schedule. Paul exhorts leaders to be diligent and to work hard. Leaders must remember that God is watching over them and assessing their work. They must not use their position of authority to impose their selfish will on others. We see an example of such a selfish will in the life of Diotrophes. Diotrophes represents the classic case of an autocratic leader. He "love[d] to have first place" as John noted (3 John 9). He even slandered the apostle John and always insisted on his own way in the church so that those who disagreed with him were kicked out of the church (3 John 10)!

Leaders are to avoid the example of Diotrophes, and they must continue to listen to those whom they are leading, for leaders are prone to trust in themselves and to think they know all the answers. How many leaders have gotten in trouble this way!

I have been struck recently how many big-time pastors in big-time churches have had to step down from their ministries. Why? They exercised their leadership in abusive, ungodly, unhelpful ways. There wasn't a check on their authority. Yes, leaders are to lead, and we desperately need leaders; but they must continue to crucify the flesh daily to lead in a way that glorifies God and helps the church.

Third, those with the gift of mercy should exercise their gift with cheerfulness. All of us are to show mercy to others, but some have a particular gift of showing mercy. If that is your gift, you should be constantly helping others, but if you continue to help others, there is the danger of growing tired and of starting to grumble about how much you are doing to assist others. Sometimes those with such a gift need to rethink their schedules to avoid burning out by failing to find periods of refreshment and rest.

On the other hand, wrong motivations may begin to pollute the gift of mercy. We may want others to notice how much we are giving, and the praise of people will not provide the joy and strength needed to show mercy to others. We will only show true mercy if we depend upon the grace of God. If you show mercy because you are conscious of God showing mercy to you, your spirit of mercy will be replenished daily.

> *We are to exercise our gifts with the right attitude and the right spirit.*

What Paul says here applies to all of us. We are to exercise our gifts with the right attitude and the right spirit. We need a fresh outpouring of God's grace in Jesus Christ every day. And we are to find our place in the body of Christ, giving ourselves to others in joy, for Jesus says, "It is more blessed to give than to receive" (Acts 20:35).

Gifts Are Worthless without Love

Fifth, Paul makes it plain in 1 Corinthians 13 that gifts without love are both useless and worthless. My purpose here isn't to unpack 1 Corinthians 13:1–7 in detail, but a few observations are worth noting. We see in verses 1–3 that charismatic gifts are worthless without love. Paul says, "If I speak human or angelic tongues but do not have love, I am a noisy gong or a clanging cymbal" (1 Cor. 13:1). The Corinthians prized speaking in tongues as the height of spiritual experience. Paul was not against tongue-speaking in and of itself, but he reminds us that charismatic experiences without love are simply an irritating noise. They are like a gong or a cymbal going off loudly at the wrong time. Spiritual experiences aren't the measure of our godliness. We might think we are very close to God when we feel close to God, when powerful emotions of love sweep over us. Emotions like this are not bad; God uses such experiences in a powerful way in our lives. But we should not think we are truly close to God if we prize emotional experiences with him, but are regularly irritable, crabby, and short-tempered at home and as we interact with people.

Verse 2 makes a similar point: "If I have the gift of prophecy and understand all mysteries and all knowledge, and if I have all faith so that I can move mountains but do not have love, I am nothing." If God gave us a prophetic gift by which we were able to know all the secrets of God and all the deepest theological truths, we would still be nothing without love.

What impresses others about the prophetic gift is the knowledge conveyed by the prophet. Sometimes we think people are spiritually mature if they are intellectually gifted and know a lot about theology and the Bible. But knowing the truth without living the truth is worthless before God. People may be impressed, but God is not. The Lord never sacrifices truth at the expense of love; truth matters. But God has no regard for truth that is not accompanied by love. Too many who are faithful in their theology are known for having a critical and loveless spirit, and that spirit repels people from their theology. I know the story of a well-known theologian who was absolutely brilliant—one of the most brilliant men I had ever met—but was also well known for being critical. One of his students said to him, "But what about the love of Christ?" He said, "Oh, I don't pay attention to those sentimental and drippy views of love." Yes, there are sentimental views of love out there that don't fit with real life. Love isn't just having cuddly feelings toward others. Yet those who are gifted with particular gifts are tempted to rationalize their lack of love.

We are also told that love cannot be measured by external actions alone. Verse 3 says, "And if I give away all my possessions, and if I give over my body in order to boast but do not have love, I gain nothing" (1 Cor. 13:3).[2] Some people, even Bible-believing Christians, say that love has nothing do with emotions and relates only to actions. They say that you can't command emotions but you can command actions, and so love in the Bible relates only to actions. But what Paul writes here clearly contradicts this idea. We might think that anyone who gives all his possessions to the poor or sacrifices his life is full of love. And certainly there is nothing externally wrong with such actions. They are commendable in and of themselves. But such actions are not loving if the motives are wrong. Someone may give to the poor to be honored by others. Someone may even sacrifice his life to be praised by others. Such actions are not loving, for love involves right affections and right motivations in the heart.

We see clearly in the following verses (1 Cor. 13:4–7) that love involves emotions, for love Paul tells us is not jealous, and jealousy is an emotion. Love is not provoked and irritated, and irritation is an emotion. Indeed, God commands us to refrain from unrighteous anger, and anger is an emotion. Yes, God gives us commands that relate to our emotions, and he summons us to obey what we cannot obey apart from his grace.

---

[2] There is a textual variant here so that Paul may be referring to the body being burnt instead of boasting. The issue is difficult and won't be adjudicated here.

Commands like this remind us that without Christ we can do nothing. Commands like this cause us to cry out to God to help us. Commands like this teach us that we need the Holy Spirit. We can't love the way the Lord calls us to love if we are not filled with the Spirit, if we don't walk by the Spirit, if we are not led by the Spirit, if we don't march in step with the Spirit, if we don't sow to the Spirit.

In verses 4–7 Paul describes the *character* of love, and describes what love looks like. It is striking that Paul uses verbs, which doesn't come across in English translations, in describing God's love. A meditative reading of Jonathan Edwards's book *Charity and Its Fruits*, which is a series of sermons on 1 Corinthians 13, would be fitting for all of us. A few brief comments should suffice here.

Patience means our schedule and our agenda don't take precedence over others, and we show patience when we love others enough to listen even when we don't feel like listening. I have been in many meetings over the years and sometimes get impatient. I think we've talked about a subject long enough and am ready to move on. But I have realized over the years that I need to be more patient with others. Part of what it means to love is to listen to what others want to talk about, to let others process and think through what concerns them.

When we are kind, we treat others with dignity, respect, and concern. It is easy, for instance, to take for granted people who are in service industries, whether they serve us at stores, when we go out to eat, at airports, etc. But they are made in the image of God too. We can view them as objects and forget that they also have worries, stresses, and concerns in their daily lives.

Jealousy and envy (1 Cor. 13:5) are not talked about a lot today, but they are responsible for many sins. We are more tempted to envy those who do the same work as us. If you are a painter, you will be more tempted to criticize another painter, if a preacher another preacher, if a lawyer another lawyer, if a receptionist another receptionist, and if a mom another mom. We are inclined to criticize those who are in the same line of work precisely because we are jealous and envious of the other's success. Our criticism is an attempt to bring our competitor down a peg. And when we criticize someone else, we often feel better ourselves.

Jonathan, Saul's son, stands out as someone who was not jealous. He could have easily hated David since David was to receive the kingdom that Jonathan should have, according to normal ancient practice, inherited. But instead of Jonathan being jealous of David, he rejoiced in what God was doing through him and was his greatest supporter. By way of contrast, Joseph's brothers could not stand the idea that he would be greater than they, and we see the consequence of jealousy: lying, treachery, and grief.

We also see that love is not self-promoting (13:5). Pride leads to self-promotion (13:4). The word for boasting and bragging Paul uses could be translated "windbag" (*perperoumai*) and the next one is literally translated "puffed up" (*physioō*). In our society, people often advertise how great they are. We used to believe the proverb that says others should praise us instead of our own lips (Prov. 27:2), but nowadays self-praise is common. We often see people praising themselves on social media. It isn't fitting to quote ourselves or to advertise how beautiful or smart we are. We think of Moses, and Numbers 12:3 tells us he was the humblest man on the earth. He was not into self-promotion, but God-promotion. We won't be meek and humble if we don't stand in God's presence, if we aren't in regular fellowship with him, if we aren't spending our time in his Word, and if we are neglecting spending time with other believers. We often think of our lives individually, but one means for growing in humility is regularly coming to church where we hear the preaching of the Word and sing God's praises with other believers. Some days these activities may not move us much. Every Sunday won't be a mountaintop experience, but little habits actually help us. Step by step, Sunday by Sunday, we are actually climbing the mountain. As we meet with other believers, we grow in the knowledge of God. When you come to church, love means that you look for ways to build up and encourage others who are present. You are willing to sing some songs you don't enjoy if others in the church are helped by them. You look out for the lonely, neglected, or you talk to the person who is not so interesting or enjoyable.

Instead of being self-centered, love is others-centered. Love "is not rude" (1 Cor. 13:5). Love has good manners. Manners vary from culture to culture, but good manners are part and parcel of love. Our society is becoming incredibly coarse and crude, but love considers what is fitting in social contexts. What passes for authenticity may just be bad manners. "Love is not irritable" (13:5). There are homes and churches where Christ is confessed, but there is constant irritation at little things that annoy us. The constant gnawing and mawing at one another contradicts our profession of faith. Churches and homes that have good doctrine but regularly display irritation and lack joy in everyday life turn people away from Jesus Christ.

We also read that love "does not keep a record of wrongs" (1 Cor. 13:5). David was mistreated constantly by Saul, yet he continued to treat Saul well, to wish him well, and would not stretch out his hand against the Lord's anointed. We remember Stephen (Acts 7:60) and especially our Lord Jesus Christ (Luke 23:34), who forgave those who put them to death. Peter wanted to count how many times we should forgive, asking the Lord if he had to forgive seven times (Matt. 18:21–22), but Jesus replied, "seventy times seven." Such forgiveness never ends.

Love is also truth exalting. "Love finds no joy in unrighteousness but rejoices in the truth" (1 Cor. 13:6). Some people think of love as a sentimental feeling only, but love never compromises the truth. Our society thinks it is loving by accepting homosexuality and other perversions of human sexuality, but this is an example of rejoicing in unrighteousness. True love stands up for the truth, even if it is painful. True love sometimes says hard things. True love doesn't compromise moral norms, and declares, "It's not right to have sex with your girlfriend before you are married," and "It's not right to live together before you are married."

Finally, love is irrepressibly optimistic. Paul says in verse 7 that love "bears all things, believes all things, hopes all things, endures all things." When he says love believes all things and hopes all things, he doesn't mean that love is gullible or naïve. He means that love continues to hope and believe that God may intervene in the lives of others, for God is able to turn things around. We believe in a God who brings life out of death, in a God who raised Christ from the dead. Those of us who believe in God should be the most optimistic people in the world. No matter how bad things get, we will finally triumph.

> *Love is irrepressibly optimistic.*

Maybe it's the eighth inning and we're behind eight to nothing, but as Christians we know that we will win in the ninth. We serve a God who loves to bring life out of death. We serve a God who loves comeback victories, and the greatest example of this is the cross and resurrection!

Conclusion

We have considered five more truths about spiritual gifts in this chapter. First, gifts aren't given to edify ourselves but to build up and strengthen the church. Gifts aren't a manifestation of the self but represent God's grace in our lives for the sake of others. Second, the baptism of the Spirit isn't a gift subsequent to conversion but is given to us at conversion. The baptism of the Spirit indicates that we belong to the church, the body of Christ. Third, the strengthening and the edification of the church comes through understanding. Ecstatic experiences without any cognitive content don't build up the church, for people are edified when they comprehend what is being said. Fourth, it is the path of wisdom to concentrate on the gifts we have. We should not ignore the gifts we don't have, but the church is helped most when we focus on the gifts God has given us. Fifth, more important than all the gifts is love, for love represents the character of God himself, and love is superior to all the gifts. The true test of spiritual maturity in our lives is whether we live in love.

Discussion Questions

1. Do you tend to think about the gifts more from a personal or corporate mind-set?

2. This chapter reminds us that "we are to exercise our gifts with the right attitude and right spirit" (p. 70). What does that look like?

3. Why is love more important than all the spiritual gifts?

Chapter Five

Questions and Answers

The topic of spiritual gifts raises many questions, and in this brief chapter, I will briefly answer six questions commonly asked about spiritual gifts: 1) Does every Christian have a spiritual gift? 2) How do we discover our gift(s)? 3) Why does Paul say to desire greater gifts if the gifts we have don't signify either inferiority or superiority? 4) Why should we seek the gifts at all, since they are sovereignly given by God? 5) Are the gifts supernatural or are they just natural talents we enjoy? 6) Are the gifts permanent possessions or can we exercise a gift that isn't normally ours?

Does Every Christian Have a Spiritual Gift?

We will take up these questions one at time. *First, does every Christian have a spiritual gift?* The Scripture is very clear on this matter so that we can say with confidence that every believer has at least one spiritual gift. Paul tells us in Romans 12:6: "we have different gifts," which implies everyone has a gift. Ephesians 4:7 is even clearer: "Now grace was given to each one of us according to the measure of Christ's gift." The words "each one of us" demonstrate that each believer is gifted. It is hard to imagine a text being much clearer than what we see in 1 Peter 4:10 where Peter says, "Just as each one has received a gift." And we see the same truth in 1 Corinthians 12:7 where Paul is clearly talking about spiritual gifts: "A manifestation of the Spirit is given to each person." Or as 1 Corinthians 12:11 says, the Spirit distributes "to each person as he wills." The entire discussion in 1 Corinthians 12 makes little sense if only some have spiritual gifts, leaving no doubt that each person has at least one spiritual gift.

How Do We Discover Our Spiritual Gifts?

Second, how do we discover our spiritual gift(s)? When I was younger, discovering one's spiritual gifts was a subject of considerable discussion, and many churches and organizations gave out tests and surveys so that members could discern their gifts. Such instruments aren't used as much anymore and for good reason. Such an abstract way of discovering our gift is actually contrary to the spirit of the New Testament, where we are summoned to give ourselves to other believers in the congregation. To put it another way, we will discover our gift when we pour ourselves into the lives of other believers, when we get involved in the life of the body.

We are to be zealous for spiritual gifts, but Paul's point isn't that we are to conduct an inventory of our own giftedness. Gifts are not granted for our own spiritual growth but for the growth of others, for the strengthening of fellow believers. Some of the spiritual gift inventories give the impression that you can discover your spiritual gift in the privacy of your room, apart from vital involvement in the body of Christ.

We can also say that in some respects it isn't crucial that you recognize and know your gift. Some worry excessively about what their gift is, and as a result they are distracted from doing actual ministry. If you are involved in the church, if you are serving other believers, you are exercising your gifts even if you don't know what they are, and that is the most important thing of all.

Why Does Paul Say to Desire the Greater Gifts?

Third, why does Paul say to desire greater gifts if the gifts we have don't signify either inferiority or superiority (1 Cor. 12:31; 14:1)? We should stop and observe that Paul exhorts believers, as noted in the previous sentence, to seek the greater gifts. This seems rather strange since he emphasized earlier in 1 Corinthians 12 that someone's gift doesn't make them inferior or superior. But if some gifts are greater than others, then isn't it the case that those who have the greater gifts are better than those who have lesser gifts? Or to put it another way: if some gifts are greater, then are those with lesser gifts inferior?

We have to pay close attention to what Paul has in mind in saying that we should desire the greater gifts. We see in 1 Corinthians 14:1–5 that some gifts are greater than others because some gifts are more edifying to the church. Paul isn't contradicting what he said earlier about people being superior or inferior, because he is speaking of two different things. When he says that the one who "prophesies is greater than the one who speaks in tongues" (1 Cor. 14:5), he isn't saying that the one who prophesies is a better person, or more spiritual, or more godly than the one who speaks in tongues. He is simply saying that the gift of prophecy is more useful in the church because people are edified more through the use of that gift. Functionally, the gift of prophecy is more helpful in the church than tongues because people are edified through words that are understood. Still, all gifts in the body are necessary. Thus a person with the gift of prophecy isn't *essentially* better than the one who lacks that gift, nor is the person with the prophetic gift more spiritual than the person with the gift of tongues. He or she doesn't have more value as a person. If someone has a gift that doesn't edify others as much as, say, the gift of prophecy, that doesn't mean they are inferior. Paul didn't believe he was necessarily more spiritually mature or godlier than a person who had the gift of helps. Some gifts are better *functionally*, in that they build up and strengthen the body, but it doesn't follow from this that the persons with such gifts have more value, dignity, and worth than those who don't have the same gift. Nor does it follow that the other gifts are unneeded.

Why Seek Gifts If They Are Sovereignly Given?

Fourth, why should we seek gifts at all, since they are sovereignly given by God? We saw earlier that the gifts one has are sovereignly given by God himself. In 1 Corinthians 12:8–9 the gifts of believers stem from the Holy Spirit. Paul tells us that the Spirit distributes the gifts "to each person as he wills" (1 Cor. 12:11), and that "God has arranged each one of the parts in the body just as he wanted" (1 Cor. 12:18). He declares in 1 Corinthians 12:28 that "God has appointed" whether one is an apostle, prophet, teacher, etc. There is no doubt, then, that God sovereignly assigns the gifts we possess.

But if this is the case, why are believers exhorted to "desire the greater gifts" (1 Cor. 12:31) and to "desire spiritual gifts, and especially that you may prophesy" (1 Cor. 14:1)? If God sovereignly decides what to give us, it seems pointless to seek for particular gifts.

One response could be that we desire the greater gifts corporately and not individually. In other words, we don't necessarily pray that we individually would exercise the greater gifts, but we ask that such gifts would be present in the congregation. Such a reading may be correct, though I am hesitant to posit such a sharp dichotomy between the individual and the corporate. Even if it is correct, however, the question still stands, for God would still sovereignly determine which persons in the congregation have the greater gifts, and thus the question of why we should seek for such gifts still applies.

The answer to this question is one of the most important themes in the Scriptures. Many go astray because of a wrong understanding of the relationship between the sovereignty of God and the responsibility of human beings. We are reminded that our spiritual gifts are the result of God's grace and sovereignty. We deserve no credit or glory for the gifts we have. They truly are gifts, so no boasting is permissible. At the same time, the Scriptures never apply the truth about God's sovereignty in such a way as to cancel out human responsibility. The Scriptures never say anything like, "God has willed such and such to happen, and so you don't need to do anything."

God uses and ordains means to reach certain ends. For instance, God has elected who will be saved before the world began (Eph. 1:4), but at the same time believers are commanded to proclaim the gospel to every person (Matt. 28:18–20), and we are to pray for the salvation of unbelievers (Rom. 10:1; 1 Tim. 2:1–2). Nowhere do Peter and Paul in their speeches in Acts ask the elect to come forward for salvation! Instead, they regularly call on their hearers to repent and believe in the gospel.

They did not think that divine sovereignty cancelled out human responsibility. In the same way, it was predestined that Jesus die on the cross for the salvation of sinners (Acts 2:23; 4:27–28), but those who put Jesus to death are indicted for their guilt. The fact that an event (Jesus' death) was willed by God doesn't rule out the authenticity and responsibility of human decisions. "Our God is in heaven and does whatever he pleases" (Ps. 115:3), but we also pray "Your kingdom come. Your will be done on earth as it is in heaven" (Matt. 6:10–11). God's will shall be done on earth, but we continue to pray that God's purposes will be fully realized. Such an explanation, of course, doesn't answer every question we have, though what the Scriptures teach are quite clear that both divine sovereignty and human responsibility are true. The same principle is present in the command to desire spiritual gifts. God sovereignly gives the gifts, but we are still to seek them.

> *God sovereignly gives the gifts, but we are still to seek them.*

Are Spiritual Gifts Supernatural or Natural?

Fifth, are spiritual gifts supernatural, or are they natural talents we enjoy? We could reply that the question is flawed, for all gifts are from God and in that sense *supernatural*. "What do you have that you have not received?" (1 Cor. 4:7). Nor is any gift exercised apart from the animating work of the Spirit, as we saw in 1 Corinthians 12:4, 8–9. There is absolutely no room, according to Paul, for a gift that is effective because of the native talent or ability of human beings, as if honor belongs to those with such remarkable abilities. Any good effect from gifts comes from God "who works all things in all" (1 Cor. 12:6 NASB).

On the other hand, it is evident that some gifts are more overtly miraculous than others. The Corinthians became entranced with the gift of tongues, not the gift of helps! Some gifts, such as tongues, interpretation of tongues, healing, miracles, and prophecy, are striking manifestations of God's presence in a community. The Corinthians were entranced with the gift of tongues, and we are not surprised, for the gift was a wonderful and astonishing indication of God's presence among his people.

Gifts such as teaching, helps, leading, giving, mercy, and exhortation are not as remarkable to the human eye, though they are still supernatural in the sense that they are animated by the Holy Spirit, and any good effect is also from the Spirit. It seems likely that some of the latter gifts are stitched into one's personality in a way that gifts like tongues and miracles are not. But the supernatural character of the gift is not thereby denied, for even in this case the gift comes from God. And the good that results from the exercise of the gift comes from the Holy Spirit, not our native talent.

Are the Gifts Permanent Possessions?

Sixth, are the gifts permanent possessions, or can we exercise a gift that isn't normally ours? Paul doesn't specifically answer this question, and so we must content ourselves with reading the clues from his writings. The emphasis seems to lie upon gifts as permanent possessions. In 1 Corinthians 12 the text moves from the gift manifested (e.g., prophecy) to gifted persons (prophets), suggesting that those who prophesy, at least usually, are prophets. Since Paul refers to prophets, evangelists, and pastor-teachers (Eph. 4:11), it seems fair to infer that the gifts of prophecy, evangelism, and teaching were a regular feature in the life of some individuals.

On the other hand, Paul doesn't refer to anyone as a healer, miracle-worker, tongue-speaker, or interpreter of tongues. He only refers to the gift itself. It doesn't follow from this that no one regularly exercised gifts like tongues or healings, but we can't rule out the idea that someone might speak in tongues or do a miracle only once or on rare occasions. But if that is the case, then they don't really have the gift of tongues; they just speak in tongues occasionally. A particular person could only claim to have a gift like healing or miracles if such manifestations are a regular occurrence in their lives. One can scarcely claim a gift of healing if they are rarely involved in healing.

Closely related to the previous question is whether Paul speaks of offices in using terms like apostles, prophets, teachers, etc. The English word "office" suggests an appointment to a certain position. It is doubtful, though, that such an idea is intended in the listing of the various gifted persons. When Paul describes someone as a prophet, he doesn't envision the appointment to a definite prophetic office, as if it is an official position in the church. A person is called a prophet because he or she regularly functions as a prophet. Of course, a teacher or a prophet may still have an office in the church, but the terms "teacher" or "prophet" don't, in and of themselves, designate an office. Instead, these terms denote a regular function.

The issue is more complicated in the case of "apostles." It seems hard to deny that Paul viewed apostleship as an office. Even if those who are called apostles inhabit an office, which is likely, apostles function as the exception, not the rule.

Conclusion

In this chapter I have tried to answer some common questions about spiritual gifts. There are, of course, many other questions that could be asked. Many believers ask about the gift of prophecy and the gift of tongues and whether gifts are still for today, and the following chapters will examine these issues.

Discussion Questions

1. Does every Christian have a spiritual gift?

2. What are some helpful and some not-so-helpful ways to discover our spiritual gifts?

3. How do we go about seeking the gifts, even as we know God is sovereign over them?

Chapter Six

What Is the Gift of Prophecy?

Earlier we defined the various gifts, but we didn't define prophecy or the gift of tongues. The reason for this is that the meaning of these two gifts is heavily disputed. In this chapter we will consider the gift of prophecy and try to determine what it is.

Prophecy Isn't Charismatic Exegesis or Preaching

Some have said that prophecy is charismatic exegesis,[1] which is defined as Spirit-driven interpretation of biblical texts.[2] This view should be rejected because it isn't clear that

---

[1] E. Earle Ellis, "The Role of the Christian Prophet in Acts," W. Ward Gasque and Ralph P. Martin, eds., *Apostolic History and the Gospel: Biblical and Historical Essays Presented to F. F. Bruce. Exeter* (The Paternoster Press, 1970), 130–44.

[2] My thanks to Richard Blaylock who wrote an excellent paper on prophecy in one of my doctoral seminars. His paper is much more

prophets were engaged in *interpreting Scripture*. They gave oracular pronouncements, words of the Lord; they were not dependent *on texts* in proclaiming the word of the Lord. I am not arguing that the revelation given by prophets is necessarily disconnected from the text of Scripture. Sometimes, as in Daniel 9, the prophecy given or the revelation spoken helps the readers understand a previous prophecy. Still, the fundamental function of prophets isn't to unpack and explain already-written biblical texts. Their prophecy may help explain previous revelation, but their words aren't a sustained explanation and exposition of biblical texts, even when they draw on previous texts in their prophecies.

Another view that has been popular in the history of the church is that prophecy is preaching. We see this interpretation in a book on preaching by the great Puritan William Perkins titled *The Art of Prophesying*.[3] A number of scholars in our day have a similar view.[4]

---

technical and thorough than my comments here.

[3] William Perkins, *The Art of Prophesying with The Calling of the Ministry*, ed. Sinclair B. Ferguson, rev. ed., Puritan Paperbacks (Edinburgh: Banner of Truth, 1996).

[4] David Hill, *New Testament Prophecy* (Atlanta: John Knox, 1979), 128; Ralph P. Martin, *The Spirit and the Congregation: Studies in 1 Corinthians 12–15* (Grand Rapids, MI: Eerdmans, 1984), 14; David E. Garland, *1 Corinthians* (Grand Rapids, MI: Baker Academic, 2003), 632. Thomas Gilliespie's view (Thomas W. Gilliespie, *The First Theologians: A Study in Early Christians Prophecy* [Grand Rapids, MI:

Those with the gift of prophecy declare God's word, though it should be distinguished from what we call preaching since it isn't from a prepared text. There are places in the Scriptures where the verb *prophesy* is used to denote speaking God's word, and yet the one speaking isn't necessarily a prophet. For example, Saul prophesied, but he certainly wasn't a prophet (1 Sam. 10:11; 19:23–24), at least not in any regular sense. So too, when Luke says that both your sons and daughters will prophesy (Acts 2:17–18), it probably means that both men and women will declare God's word, but it doesn't necessitate that they are all prophets, that they all have the spiritual gift of prophecy. Those who prophecy may speak forth God's word (and in that sense it is similar to preaching), but it differs from preaching and the gift of teaching since the one who speaks isn't working from a written text; they are not expositing and explaining the Word of God.[5]

Eerdmans, 1994], 28) that prophecy is gospel exposition in Paul is a rather similar reading.

[5] It isn't my purpose to develop this thought here. See the fascinating essay by Iain M. Duguid, "What Kind of Prophecy Continues? Defining the Difference between Continuationism and Cessationism," in *Redeeming the Life of the Mind: Essays in Honor of Vern Poythress*, ed. John M. Frame, Wayne Grudem, and John J. Hughes (Wheaton, IL: Crossway, 2017), 112–28. Duguid points to a number of examples where there are different kinds of prophets, what he calls capital *P* and small *p* prophets. This is an area that warrants further explanation, and there are some distinctions which warrant more discussion than is

I conclude that prophecy doesn't fit with what we call preaching today since those who preach rely on a text of Scripture and explain and apply what the Scriptures teach. Those who prophesy, however, don't proclaim God's word from a written text but convey what God has revealed to them. Prophecy, then, isn't the same thing as preaching, though it can overlap in some respects with the function of preaching, since those who prophesy may declare and apply God's will to people in particular situations.

Prophets Receive Spontaneous Revelation from God

The feature that separates prophecy from teaching is that those who prophesy communicate revelations from God. We receive help from 1 Corinthians 14:6, "So now, brothers and sisters, if I come to you speaking in other tongues, how will I benefit you unless I speak to you with a revelation or knowledge or prophecy or teaching?" The word *knowledge* is another way of referring to "teaching," i.e., knowledge is the fruit and consequence of teaching. So too, the word "revelation" is another way of referring to "prophecy," in that the consequence of receiving a prophecy is a revelation given by God. The revelation given is spontaneous in that it isn't derived through studying

---

possible here. I am not convinced, however, that the small *p* prophet erred in their prophecies.

the biblical text or any traditional material. God communicates his word directly to the mind of the prophet. The prophet may not communicate immediately what God has revealed, but the revelation itself is spontaneous.

We see the spontaneous nature of prophecy in 1 Corinthians 14:29–30. A prophet is speaking in the congregation, but suddenly a revelation is given to another prophet. The first prophet should then sit down and allow the prophet who just received a revelation to speak.

Those who prophesy communicate revelations from God.

We see other indications of the spontaneous character of prophecy in Acts 11:27–28. Agabus wasn't studying Scripture and trying to unfold its meaning to his hearers. The Lord revealed to him that a famine would arise in the Roman world. In the same way, Agabus predicted that the Jews would bind Paul and hand him over to the Gentiles (Acts 21:10–11). Here we see prophecy at work: a revelation is given to Agabus about what would happen to Paul.

We should not conclude from the accounts about Agabus that prophecy is always predictive, for prophecy may address present circumstances as well. We read in Acts 13:1–3 about various people who gathered to fast and to worship the Lord. While they were worshiping, the Lord spoke, almost certainly through a prophetic oracle: "Set apart for me Barnabas and Saul for the work to which I have called them" (Acts 13:2).

God revealed spontaneously to those who were gathered that Paul and Barnabas should go on a missionary journey. Thus, those who teach explain a biblical text, but prophecy reveals a message from God, and prophets receive it directly from God in a spontaneous way.

The revelatory character of prophecy is also evident in 1 Corinthians 13:2, where we read, "If I have the gift of prophecy and understand all mysteries and all knowledge." The verse is clearly hyperbolic since no prophet understands *all* mysteries, nor does any prophet have *all* knowledge. Still, the word *mysteries* helps us to grasp the nature of prophecy, for those who prophesy bring to light what is hidden and reveal what isn't accessible to ordinary human beings.

We see something similar in 1 Corinthians 14:24–25 where one who prophesies may say something that uncovers the "secrets of [the] heart," showing again the revelatory character of prophecy. We also read in 1 Corinthians 14:3 that those who prophesy speak "to people for their strengthening, encouragement, and consolation." We should not use this verse alone to define the nature of prophecy, for certainly people are strengthened, encouraged, and comforted through other gifts as well. Paul does, however, contrast prophecy with uninterpreted tongues to show us that prophecy stands out as a declaration of God's revelation, and this revelation is received spontaneously.

Conclusion

In this chapter I have argued that prophecy is the reception of spontaneous revelations that are communicated to God's people. Prophecy isn't the same thing as preaching since those who preach exposit the biblical text, though it can overlap with preaching in that prophets may exhort and encourage God's people with God's word. Nor is prophecy the same thing as charismatic exegesis, but this isn't to say that prophets don't take into account previous scriptural texts in their prophecies. What marks prophecy out, however, is the reception of spontaneous revelations from God, and such words instruct, encourage, and warn the people of God.

Discussion Questions

1. What do you think are some common misperceptions about prophecy?

2. How would you define prophecy after reading this chapter?

Chapter Seven

Is New Testament Prophecy Mixed with Error?

A very common prescript to the words of Old Testament prophets was, "Thus says the LORD." These Old Testament prophets functioned as God's mouthpiece to his people; his exact words came directly through them. In fact, the test of whether one was truly a prophet of God was whether his words came to pass (Deut. 18:21–22). If they did not, he was to be regarded as a false prophet.

One view—a very common one today—asserts that New Testament prophecy is different from Old Testament prophecy in this regard. While Old Testament prophecy was infallible, many assert that the gift of prophecy referred to in the New Testament—and discussed in the last chapter—is fallible and mixed with error. I will argue in this chapter that the idea that New Testament prophecies are mixed with error is mistaken.

Arguments Supporting the Fallibility of New Testament Prophecy

Wayne Grudem is the most famous and persuasive advocate of this view. He deems Old Testament prophecy to be infallible and inerrant, but New Testament prophecy to be fallible. Under the old covenant genuine prophets were identified by their accuracy. We are told, for instance, about the prophet Samuel that "the LORD was with him and let none of his words fall to the ground" (1 Sam. 3:19 ESV). Notice that *all* of Samuel's words were fulfilled, and there was no instance where he prophesied falsely. Those who think New Testament prophecy is mixed with error claim that the successors to the Old Testaments prophets are the apostles, and thus the apostles were without error in what they taught, but the words of New Testament prophets contain a mixture of truth and error.

Why do some believe New Testament prophecy is different from Old Testament prophecy? To put it another way, why do some argue that New Testament prophecy is a mixture of truth and error?[1]

---

[1] To be clear, the argument is that the prophecy God gives is infallible, but it becomes tainted with error in reception or transmission.

First, they point out that the *prophecies* are judged, not the *prophets*. We read in 1 Corinthians 14:29, "Two or three prophets should speak, and the others should evaluate." Why are the prophecies evaluated? To separate the truth from error in the prophecies given. Thus, the prophecies—and not the prophets—are evaluated.

We see the same thing in 1 Thessalonians 5:20–21 where Paul says, "Don't despise prophecies, but test all things. Hold on to what is good." The church should not reject the prophetic gift, but at the same time they should test the prophecies, because the prophecies might have mistakes in them. Believers should test and evaluate the prophecies, retaining what is good and rejecting any errors.

A second argument in support of the idea that prophecies can be mixed with error is that some New Testament prophecies are disobeyed, and such disobedience isn't sinful. We read in Acts 21:4, "Through the Spirit they told Paul not to go to Jerusalem." Paul, however, did not heed these words (Acts 21:13–14), and did not think the prophecy represented God's word to him. Luke doesn't conclude that Agabus was a false prophet, nor does he give any indication that Paul sinned by failing to follow the advice not to go to Jerusalem. In fact, Paul was led by the Spirit to go to Jerusalem (Acts 19:21; 20:22). It seems, then, that prophecy may be mixed with error, but the person who says something errant isn't identified as a false prophet. In the Old Testament, of course, errors in prophecy would confirm that one was a false prophet.

Third, it is also argued that Agabus's prophecy about Paul being handed over to the Romans by the Jews was in error. Agabus "came to us, took Paul's belt, tied his own feet and hands, and said, 'This is what the Holy Spirit says: "In this way the Jews in Jerusalem will bind the man who owns this belt and deliver him over to the Gentiles"'" (Acts 21:11). If we read the story of what happened to Paul in Acts 21, the Jews didn't actually bind Paul and hand him over to the Romans. Instead, they seized Paul in the temple, carried him outside the temple gates, started beating him, and attempted to kill him. The Roman tribune, Claudius Lysias, alerted to what was happening, sent his troops to break up the disturbance, rescuing Paul from the hands of the Jews. The Jews didn't hand Paul over to the Romans; the Romans rescued Paul from the Jews! Agabus, then, got the details wrong in his prophecy; his prophecy was a mixture of truth and error. Still, Agabus wasn't rejected as a false prophet.

What do proponents of this view make of Ephesians 2:20 which says that the church "is built on the foundation of the apostles and prophets"? The verse is important because it suggests that New Testament prophets have the same authority as the apostles. Grudem argues that the prophets here should not be understood as separate from the apostles. Instead, in this instance the apostles and prophets are the same entity since both nouns are under the same Greek article.[2] Paul refers, then, to apostles who are also prophets.

New Testament Prophecy Is Authoritative and Infallible

Despite the arguments supporting the notion that New Testament prophecy differs from Old Testament prophecy in that it is mixed with error, the arguments to the contrary are more convincing. In other words, New Testament prophecy doesn't differ from Old Testament prophecy, and like Old Testament prophecy, it is infallible and always true. New Testament prophecies aren't mixed with errors. Several arguments support this position.

First, we expect New Testament prophecy to be like Old Testament prophecy unless there are decisive reasons for saying they are different. The burden of proof, in other words, belongs to those who say that New Testament prophecy is different in nature and character from Old Testament prophecy. Our natural expectation is that New Testament prophecy operates in the same way as Old Testament prophecy. Joel's promise that both the young and old will prophesy (Joel 2:28) assumes that the nature is the same in both Testaments. We must remember that the issue of false prophets is a major

---

[2] W. A. Grudem, *The Gift of Prophecy in 1 Corinthians* (Washington, DC: University Press of America, 1982), 82–105.

issue and problem in the New Testament, just as it was in the Old Testament (cf. Rev. 2:20). Jeremiah indicts the prophets repeatedly for prophesying falsely and for saying things that aren't true (e.g., Jer. 20:6; 23:16, 25–26, 32; 27:10, 15), and they stand in contrast to genuine prophets who always speak the truth (Jer. 28:9). John warns about "many false prophets" spread abroad (1 John 4:1; cf. also Acts 13:6; 2 Pet. 1:21; 2:1), which reflects Jesus' concern about "many false prophets" rising up (Matt. 24:11; cf. Matt. 24:24; Mark 13:22; Luke 6:22). Believers are admonished to be vigilant about "false prophets who come to you in sheep's clothing" (Matt. 7:15; cf. Rev. 16:13; 19:20; 20:10). But if the word of true prophets is mixed with error, identifying false prophets would be very difficult indeed. Those who claim that New Testament prophecy is fallible don't account well for the need to discriminate between true and false prophets, for making such judgments would be terribly hard if the words of true prophets contain both truth and error.

Sometimes continuationists say that prophecy is like teaching since teachers aren't infallible, but there is a key difference between prophecy and teaching. Teachers, as noted earlier, expound and explain the biblical text. Prophets, however, bring an immediate word from God. The credibility of teachers can be examined and tested from the text they are teaching. Those hearing can assess whether what is taught accords with the authoritative text, with the argument that the biblical text is making. But when prophets speak, they aren't explaining and expositing a text. They claim a direct word from God, and thus their words can't be compared to a written text. We see, then, that the differences between prophecy and teaching are significant, and the problem with errors in prophecy is not solved by appealing to the gift of teaching.

Those who defend the idea that New Testament prophecy is mixed with error tend to restrict prophecy to individual guidance, but such a scenario is quite unlikely. New Testament prophets exercised a broad and influential ministry; they were not solely or even primarily focused on giving guidance to individual Christians. It is much more likely, then, that the way of assessing prophets is the same in the New Testament as in the Old Testament. Prophets who erred are false prophets.

Second, the significance of the ministry of New Testament prophets is evident and can't be restricted to private, individual concerns. The church is "built on the foundation of the apostles and prophets" (Eph. 2:20). The foundational role of the apostles and prophets points to the authority of their words, suggesting that prophecy in the New Testament has the same authority as prophecy in the Old Testament. If prophecy still exists today, it is hard to resist the conclusion that the foundation established by the apostles and prophets hasn't been completed, and that the New Testament prophets are still adding to the foundation of apostolic teaching.[3] Then we are faced with the situation where people are still speaking revelatory words today, and in such a scenario the final and sole authority of the New Testament is threatened. We see in Ephesians 2:20 that the words of the prophets play a decisive role in the shaping of the doctrine and life of the church.

> *If prophecy still exists today, it is hard to resist the conclusion that the foundation established by the apostles and prophets hasn't been completed.*

They aren't merely good advice about whom one should marry or about private matters in one's individual life. They play a foundational role in establishing the church of Jesus Christ!

Incidentally, there is no doubt that New Testament prophets are in mind in Ephesians 2:20, and this is confirmed by Ephesians 3:5, where Paul says the mystery "was not made known to people in other generations as it is *now* revealed to his holy apostles and prophets by the Spirit." The mystery is that Jews and Gentiles are equal members in the church in Jesus Christ (Eph. 3:6), and it is obvious that this truth was not disclosed to Old Testament prophets with the

---

[3] Grudem, of course, doesn't think such is happening, but I am arguing that the implication of the New Testament texts points away from Grudem's reading.

same clarity granted to the apostles and New Testament prophets. Indeed, the order of the words (apostles and then prophets) confirms that New Testament prophets are intended, since we would expect the order to be prophets and apostles if Old Testament prophets were the referent.

We have seen, however, that Grudem thinks that only one group is in view in Ephesians 2:20: the apostles *who are also* prophets. The interpretation proposed, however, is quite unlikely and should be rejected. We see, for instance, in both Ephesians 4:11 and 1 Corinthians 12:28 that apostles and prophets are distinguished from one another. We have no other example where apostles and prophets are collapsed together like this. The most natural view is that apostles and prophets are distinguished in Ephesians 2:20 as well.[4] Since the apostles and prophets are distinguished from one another, the prophets along with the apostles play a crucial role in the establishing of the church of Jesus Christ. But it is hard to conceive of prophets playing such a fundamental role if their prophecies are mixed with error. It is more convincing to conclude that the

---

[4] Grudem appeals to the Granville Sharp rule where two nouns with a singular article refer to the same entity. The problem with appealing to this rule is that the Granville Sharp rule only applies to singular nouns, not plural ones. Since we have plural nouns here, there is no basis grammatically for thinking that they refer to the same entity. We should try to discern why there is one article with both nouns, and the best answer is that the apostles and prophets together constitute the foundation of the church.

New Testament prophets have the same authority and infalli-
bility as Old Testament prophets.

Third, we have seen that in 1 Corinthians 14:29 and
1 Thessalonians 5:20–21 that the prophecies given by New
Testament prophets are evaluated and judged. Those who think
New Testament prophets can err argue that it is the *prophecies*
that are evaluated, *not the prophets*. But this distinction isn't
persuasive, for the only basis by which Old Testament prophets
could be assessed was their prophecies. We saw in Deuteronomy
18:21–22 that the genuineness of Old Testament prophets is
determined by whether *their prophecies* come true. When we
read 1 Corinthians 14:29 and 1 Thessalonians 5:20–21, the
same criteria applies. There is no other way to determine if
a prophet is authentic apart from the words they speak; they
are shown to be false prophets, just as in the Old Testament, if
their prophecies err.

Paul doesn't need to expand upon the admonition since the
readers knew from the Old Testament itself that false prophets are exposed by their errant prophecies. Readers are warned
about the danger of false prophets in 1 John 4:1, "Dear friends,
do not believe every spirit, but test the spirits to see if they are
from God, because many false prophets have gone out into the
world."

Sometimes people bring up the issue of whether every prophetic word is written down and included in the Scriptures.
They say that if prophecies were entirely true and authoritative

they would need to be written down and preserved in the Scriptures. Actually, such an objection is baseless and says nothing about the nature of New Testament prophecy. Even Old Testament prophecies didn't have to be written down and preserved to be true and authoritative. In fact, many prophecies—indeed most—aren't part of the Scriptures, but such a state of affairs doesn't indicate that prophecies that weren't written down contained errors. Everything Elijah and Elisha said when they were speaking in the name of the Lord was true, but most of what they prophesied hasn't been preserved in the Scriptures.[5] We have no record what the fifty prophets hidden by Obadiah prophesied (1 Kings 18:4). Nor do we know the prophecies of the sons of the prophets who were associated especially with Elisha (2 Kings 2:3, 5, 7, 15; 4:1, 38; 5:22; 6:1; 9:1). Both of these groups must have prophesied since they are called prophets. But *nothing* that the sons of the prophets prophesied is contained in Scripture. Still, *everything* they prophesied was true! They didn't make mistakes in their prophecies even if their words haven't been preserved for all time. Notice that we have the words of at least sixty prophets in these two examples that were not written down or saved for

---

[5] We should not understand the prophets to be without error in everything they said during their lives. They were ordinary human beings! But when they spoke in the Lord's name, their words were without error.

posterity, showing that prophecies don't have to be included in Scripture to be completely true.

We have no indication, then, that New Testament prophecy differs from Old Testament prophecy in terms of its complete accuracy simply because prophecies weren't written down for posterity. New Testament prophets spoke authoritatively and with complete truth to the situations in their churches. The fact that most prophecies weren't written down and preserved is completely irrelevant as far as the truth of the prophecies is concerned. It is a category mistake to think that if prophecies are without error, then they must be written down and included in the Scriptures. And it doesn't logically follow that prophecies must contain errors if they aren't preserved and written down. God spoke authoritatively and truly through the prophets, even if their prophecies weren't recorded and preserved. They spoke the infallible word of God to their contemporaries, who needed to hear these true and authoritative words of God.

Fourth, Paul's claim that his word is superior to the prophets in 1 Corinthians 14:37–38 doesn't suggest that prophecies may contain errors. He addresses the potential situation where someone who *claims* or *thinks* (*dokei*) he is a prophet ignores what Paul commands. If a prophet "ignores" what Paul says, then the prophet is "ignored" by God himself (1 Cor. 14:38)! The issue here isn't whether the words of the prophets are mixed with error. Instead, the issue is whether one is a false prophet! Those who claim to be prophets and who yet ignore

Paul's words are ignored by God, which means they do not belong to Jesus Christ and are not true prophets. Paul isn't just giving a slight slap on the wrist here, but admonishes those who claim to be prophets that their words must not and cannot contravene his apostolic authority. If they claim to have a message from God that contradicts Paul, they are not part of the Christian church.

Fifth, the notion that Agabus was mistaken in Acts 21:11, when he said that the Jews would bind Paul and deliver him over to the Romans, is unconvincing. We need to remind ourselves that his prophecy about the famine was completely accurate (Acts 11:28), and the same is true regarding his prophecy about Paul. On first glance we might think Agabus was mistaken regarding Paul's arrest (Acts 21:11) since Paul was rescued by the Romans from the hands of the Jews who were pommeling him. But we need to beware about interpreting the fulfillment of prophecy in a rigid way. Actually, when Paul was imprisoned in Rome and recounted to Jews there about his arrest in Jerusalem, he appeals to the very word Agabus used in relaying what happened to him. Agabus predicted in Acts 21:11 that the Jews would "deliver" (*paradōsousin*) Paul "over to the Gentiles." When Paul informs the Jews in Rome later what happened on that occasion, he says, "After three days he called together the leaders of the Jews. When they had gathered he said to them: 'Brothers, although I have done nothing against our people or the customs of our ancestors, I was delivered (*paredothēn*) as a prisoner from Jerusalem into the hands of the Romans'" (Acts 28:17). Apparently, Paul didn't think Agabus was mistaken since he says he was "delivered" or "handed over" by the Jews to the Romans. We might think it would have been more accurate for Paul to say he wasn't handed over but rescued. We see, however, that Paul's words indicate that he believed Agabus's prophecy was fulfilled.[6]

The fulfillment of Agabus's prophecy raises another issue that should be addressed briefly, and it relates to those of us who believe Scripture is inerrant. Modern Western conceptions of accuracy must not be applied to the Scriptures when we speak of accuracy. The Chicago Statement on Biblical Inerrancy introduces the kind of qualifications that are needed in defining the term.[7] The careful work of Craig Blomberg also demonstrates that inerrancy must be nuanced properly, that we can't impose upon the Scriptures the kind of computer

---

[6] Nor does it work to say that the allusion is actually to Acts 23, where Paul was handed over by the Jewish judicial system to the Romans after being examined by the Jews. Such a reading doesn't fit the facts, for even when Paul was interrogated by the Jews, he was under Roman authority. Furthermore, in Acts 23 the Jews didn't hand Paul over to the Romans. The tribune feared again that they might harm Paul, so he rescued Paul from their hands again.

[7] International Council on Biblical Inerrancy, "The Chicago Statement on Biblical Inerrancy," *The Journal of the Evangelical Theological Society* 21 (December 1978): 289–96.

accuracy we have in our culture today.[8] What I am saying here is that if Agabus is judged to be in error, the same kind of judgment could be used to assess other texts which some claim have errors. To avoid misunderstanding, I am not saying that those who think New Testament prophecy is mixed with errors in any way deny inerrancy! The point is that a restrictive definition of what constitutes error could also apply *in principle* to the doctrine of inerrancy. Those who think that Agabus erred define error too narrowly and rigidly.

Two other arguments point to Agabus's accuracy. Agabus uses prophetic symbolism (Acts 21:11) like the Old Testament prophets in taking Paul's belt and tying his hands and feet. We are reminded of Isaiah who walked about naked, symbolizing the judgment coming on Egypt and Cush (Isa. 20:1–6). Or, we think of Jeremiah wearing a linen undergarment, which symbolizes how Judah and Jerusalem should cling to the Lord (Jer. 13:1–11). Instead, the garment was hidden at the Euphrates, which ruined the garment, indicating Israel's distance from the Lord. Similarly, Ezekiel built miniature siege works against

---

[8] Craig Blomberg, *The Historical Reliability of the Gospels* (Downers Grove, IL: InterVarsity Press, 1987); idem, *The Historical Reliability of John's Gospel: Issues and Commentary* (Downers Grove, IL: InterVarsity Press, 2001); idem, *Can We Still Believe the Bible? An Evangelical Assessment with Contemporary Questions* (Grand Rapids: Brazos, 2014); idem, *The Historical Reliability of the New Testament: Countering the Challenges to Evangelical Christian Beliefs* (Nashville, TN: B&H Academic, 2016).

Jerusalem, which symbolized Babylon's siege of Jerusalem (Ezek. 4). The symbolism used by Agabus shows that he is in line with Old Testament prophets, that his prophecy is as truthful as theirs. The way Luke frames the prophecies of Agabus shows that Luke considered him to be in line with Old Testament prophets.

Another indication of Agabus's authority is the formula used to introduce his words. Agabus says, "This (*tade*) is what the Holy Spirit says." A similar formula is used hundreds of times in the Old Testament for authoritative words of the Lord conveyed by prophets. The word *tade*, which literally means "these things," is used repeatedly in the Old Testament to denote the authoritative words of the Lord. We find the same phenomenon in the book of Revelation where all seven letters to the seven churches are introduced with the authoritative words of Jesus Christ (Rev. 2:1, 8, 12, 18; 3:1, 7, 14). In every case, the words of Jesus are introduced with the same formula found on Agabus's lips: "these things" (*tade*). Luke gives us every indication, then, that he believed Agabus spoke just like the Old Testament prophets and like Jesus Christ himself in the book of Revelation. We have no hint that Luke thought Agabus was mistaken, and actually just the opposite is communicated. Agabus speaks the word of the Lord.

Sixth, the most difficult text for those who think prophecy in the New Testament is infallible is Acts 21:4 and 21:12–13. The people tell Paul not to go to Jerusalem "through the Spirit" since it is predicted that he will suffer there, but Paul insists on going and claims that he is led by the Spirit in his decision. Those who think New Testament prophecy is mixed with error say we have a clear example here of an error in prophecy. This interpretation is certainly possible. There wouldn't even be a debate if this matter were easy to resolve! But another reading of the evidence is more compelling, and this reading supports the notion that New Testament prophecies are infallible.

In Acts 21:4 the prophecy is correct (Paul would suffer), but the inference drawn from the prophecy (Paul shouldn't go to Jerusalem) is mistaken. I would suggest that the inference drawn from the prophecy was not part of the prophecy itself. Thus, the prophecy that Paul would face suffering in Jerusalem was accurate and Spirit-inspired; the *conclusion* that people drew from the prophecy—that Paul should not travel to Jerusalem—was mistaken. It did not derive from the Spirit. C. K. Barrett gets it right when he says, "Luke does not express himself clearly. His words taken strictly would mean either that Paul was deliberately disobedient to the will of God or that the Spirit was mistaken in the guidance given. It is unthinkable that Luke intended either of these."[9] Barrett goes on to propose the same solution offered above.

---

[9] C. K. Barrett, *Acts 15-28* (ICC; Edinburgh: T&T Clark, 1998), 990. Barrett's comment should not be misunderstood, for we don't have a criticism of Luke. It wasn't Luke's purpose to be precise here since the point of his narrative wasn't to unpack the nature of prophecy.

What about Impressions?

We have seen that there are decisive reasons for saying that New Testament prophecy, just like Old Testament prophecy, is inerrant and infallible. What most call prophecy in churches today, in my judgment, isn't the New Testament gift of prophecy, for New Testament prophecy is inerrant. We should not, however, conclude that what happens in charismatic churches today is demonic. It is better to characterize what is happening today as the sharing of *impressions* rather than prophecy. God may impress something on a person's heart and mind, and he may use such impressions to help others in their spiritual walk. It is a matter of definition; what some people call prophecies are actually impressions, where someone senses that God is leading them to speak to someone or to make some kind of statement about a situation.

> *What some people call prophecies are actually impressions.*

The word *impression* is a better description than the word *prophecy* here because impressions may be a mixture of truth and error. Sometimes, in a most remarkable way they might be completely right! God may lay something on

---

Luke assumed that his readers would agree that prophecy is always true and never in error. Barrett is exactly right in saying that it was "unthinkable" to say that the Spirit made a mistake or that Paul disobeyed God's will.

someone's heart, and it may be exactly right and exactly what a person needs to hear. Sometimes the impression may be quite astonishing and clearly miraculous, though this is quite rare. On the other hand, sometimes impressions are totally wrong, and it is evident that the words shared are neither helpful nor true. And some impressions may be a mixture of truth and error. Those whose impressions are wrong aren't false prophets. After all, in my view, impressions aren't prophecies anyway! There is a danger, of course, of relying too much on impressions, and I will say more about that shortly.

The difference between cessationists[10] and continuationists[11] is in some ways insignificant at the practical level when it comes to prophecy, for what continuationists call prophecy, cessationists call impressions. As a cessationist, I affirm that God may speak to his people through impressions. And there are occasions where impressions are startlingly accurate.

Is the debate on prophecy, then, just semantic? I don't think so, for it is important to accurately define terms that are in Scripture. In my estimation, what modern-day charismatics practice isn't the same thing as the gift of prophecy in Scripture, and it is important to have scriptural clarity on the nature of prophecy, especially since the charismatic view opens up the church to the danger of false prophets. Furthermore,

---

[10] Those who believe the gifts of tongues and prophecy have ceased.
[11] Those who believe these gifts continue.

many charismatics don't have the careful reservations and qualifications in defining prophecy that we find in excellent scholars like Wayne Grudem and Sam Storms, and these less careful
charismatics sometimes use their so-called prophecies in a way
that endangers the final and sole authority of Scripture. The
claim to have a prophecy can be used as a club or even a form
of abuse over those who are naïve or immature. Impressions
should not, therefore, be confused with prophecy.

God can use impressions for our good, but they aren't the
same thing as prophecy and need to be distinguished from
prophecy. They can't be of great importance because Scripture
doesn't address them. It doesn't follow that impressions are
useless, for we share many thoughts with others as believers
that aren't the actual words of God in conversations, in small
groups, and even in larger meetings. We don't dismiss the value
of such insights even if they are not inspired words. We are
reminded, however, that we should not overestimate impressions, and that we need to be careful so that people don't rely
on them. Jonathan Edwards rightly warns,

> I would therefore entreat the people of God to be very
> cautious how they give heed to such things. I have seen
> 'em fail in very many instances; and know by experi-
> ence that impressions being made with great power,
> and upon the minds of true saints, yea, eminent saints;
> and presently after, yea, in the midst of, extraordinary
> exercises of grace and sweet communion with God,

and attended with texts of Scripture strongly impressed on the mind, are no sure signs of their being revelations from heaven: for I have known such impressions [to] fail, and prove vain by the event, in some instances attended with all these circumstances. I know that they that leave the sure word of prophecy (the Bible), that God has given us to be a light shining in a dark place, to follow such impressions and impulses, leave the guidance of the pole star to follow a Jack-with-a-lanthorn. And no wonder therefore that sometimes they are led a dreadful dance, and into woeful extravagancies.[12]

Edwards wisely warns us about the danger of relying on impressions. Some people are quite confident by nature and confuse their own certainty with the leading of the Spirit. We see that God may use impressions, but they should not be the norm in our lives and we should not rely on them for guidance.

Conclusion

I have argued in this chapter that New Testament prophecy is not mixed with error but is infallible and inerrant, just like Old Testament prophecy. We have seen that the church is built

---

[12] Jonathan Edwards, "Distinguishing Marks of a Work of the Spirit of God" in *The Great Awakening,* in *The Works of Jonathan Edwards,* vol. 4, C. C. Goen, ed. (New Haven, CT: Yale University Press, 1972), 282.

on the foundation of the apostles and New Testament prophets. We have also seen that the claims that New Testament prophets erred aren't credible. The total truthfulness of New Testament prophets was a vital matter in the early church because false prophets were a constant danger. If New Testament prophets spoke a mixture of truth and error, discerning who were false and true prophets would have been a nightmare. Finally, we have seen that what many in charismatic circles today call prophecies are rightly labeled impressions. God may give these impressions, but they should not be received with the same level of authority as Old or New Testament prophecy.

Discussion Questions

1. Do you think Old Testament and New Testament prophecy are different in nature?

2. Why does it matter whether New Testament prophecy contains errors?

3. Discuss the implications of Ephesians 2:20 on the topic of prophecy.

4. What is the difference in prophecy and an impression?

Chapter Eight

The Nature of the Gift of Tongues

I have argued that those with the gift of prophecy communicate infallible words from God, and these divine messages are given spontaneously by God to his messengers. In doing so, I have argued that the gift of prophecy has ceased, and that what many refer to as prophetic words in our day are really impressions—some given by God, some not.

The purpose of this chapter is to investigate the nature of the gift of tongues. What is the gift? How does the Bible describe it? Do people still speak in tongues today? Many people claim to speak in tongues today, but we have to ask whether what they are doing matches the gift we find in the Bible. I will argue from Acts and 1 Corinthians that the gift of tongues is the gift of speaking in human languages. Therefore, tongue-speaking is not, as many today believe, speaking with ecstatic utterances, that is to say, speaking words with no discernible code or linguistic pattern.

Speaking in Tongues in Acts

We begin with Acts. In Acts 2, the gift of tongues is clearly human languages, because people from all over the world hear the apostles "speaking in [their] own language" (2:6), and "each one" heard them "in [their] own native language" (2:8). The apostles were declaring the works of God "in our own tongues" (2:11). A longer citation of Acts 2:6–11 clarifies that the gift here was speaking in other languages. "How is it that each of us can hear them in our own native language? Parthians, Medes, Elamites; those who live in Mesopotamia, in Judea and Cappadocia, Pontus and Asia, Phrygia and Pamphylia, Egypt and the parts of Libya near Cyrene; visitors from Rome (both Jews and converts), Cretans and Arabs—we hear them declaring the magnificent acts of God in our own tongues." Those from all different parts of the world heard the apostles speaking in their own languages.

Some have argued that the gift wasn't actually speaking but *hearing*, but this is not the most natural way to read the text. For instance, Acts 2:4 says that the 120 were "filled with the Holy Spirit and began to speak in different tongues." Acts 2:6 says the people heard them "*speaking* in [their] own language."

It seems clear, then, that the gift in Acts 2 was the ability to speak other languages.

The next instance of speaking in tongues is found in the story of Cornelius and his friends (Acts 10:1–48). They receive the Holy Spirit and speak in tongues (Acts 10:46). Luke makes it clear that the gift is the same one that was given to the 120 on Pentecost. In other words, Cornelius and his friends spoke in languages they didn't know. Peter confirms this interpretation in Acts 11:17 when he says, "If, then, God gave them the *same* gift that he also gave to us." Peter specifically tells us that the gift was the same one received on Pentecost. The tongue-speaking by the Ephesian twelve in Acts 19:6 should be interpreted similarly, for Luke hasn't given us any indication to the contrary.

Speaking in Tongues in 1 Corinthians

It seems quite clear that tongues in Acts refers to speaking in languages unknown by the speaker, but many interpreters think that speaking in tongues in 1 Corinthians 12–14 refers to speaking in ecstatic utterances instead of in other languages. We read, for instance, in 1 Corinthians 14:2, "For the person who speaks in another tongue is not speaking to people but to God, since no one understands him; he speaks mysteries in the Spirit." Many think Paul must be referring to speaking in ecstatic utterances, for unlike what we find in Acts the speech

125

is directed to God, and not to human beings. The "mysteries" spoken, according to this interpretation, refer to ecstatic speech, and some maintain the verse only makes sense if Paul has ecstatic utterances in mind. Many also see a reference to ecstatic utterance in the "tongues of angels" (1 Cor. 13:1), which seems to indicate that there is tongue-speaking that isn't confined to human languages.

The argument for ecstatic utterances is possible but not convincing. First, tongues can't be interpreted unless they have a code that can be deciphered. Gibberish and ecstatic babbling can't be interpreted since there is nothing to be communicated in random vocalization. Indeed, the word *tongue* (*glōssa*) points to a language, to some kind of code.[1] As we have noted, many see a case for ecstatic utterances in the phrase "tongues of angels" (1 Cor. 13:1), but the case for ecstatic utterances should not be made from this phrase. First of all, even the tongues of angels have to be interpreted and thus must be in some kind of code, but the ecstatic utterances of today lack any kind of code and aren't translatable. Linguists can't discern a pattern that points to languages. Of course, one can always argue that the code people speak in today lacks any linguistic pattern and yet there is a code decipherable only by God and only by those able to

---

[1] Gordon D. Fee, *The First Epistle to the Corinthians*, rev. ed. (Grand Rapids, MI: Eerdmans, 2014), 597–98; D. A. Carson, *Showing the Spirit: A Theological Exposition of 1 Corinthians 12–14* (Grand Rapids, MI: Baker, 1987), 77–88.

interpret tongues. Such a scenario is really impossible to prove, but it seems like an unlikely and forced conclusion.

Second, even if there is a distinct tongue of angels, it isn't clear that the Corinthians spoke in the tongues of angels, for the reference to the tongues of angels is probably rhetorical on Paul's part. Seeing the tongues of angels as a rhetorical flourish is supported by 1 Corinthians 13:2, for here Paul certainly resorts to hyperbole, when he says that one who has the gift of prophecy understands "*all* mysteries" and "*all* knowledge." Obviously, only God knows all mysteries and all knowledge, and so the reference to all mysteries and knowledge is hyperbolic. The same is likely true with reference to the tongues of angels. The argument that tongues of angels refers to ecstatic utterances, then, doesn't fit.

A stronger argument for ecstatic utterances is 1 Corinthians 14:2 since Paul says that tongue speakers don't speak to people but to God, and they utter mysteries in or by the Spirit. After all, those in Acts understood immediately those speaking in tongues, but in 1 Corinthians they don't understand without an interpreter. In Acts the gift of tongues is connected to prophecy (Acts 2:16–18), but in 1 Corinthians 14:1–5 Paul distinguishes it from prophecy. In 1 Corinthians 14:20–23 he says tongues bring judgment, but in Acts 2 they result in people being saved! In Acts the gospel is proclaimed evangelistically, but in 1 Corinthians those who speak in tongues praise the Lord and exclusively edify believers.

Despite the popularity of this interpretation, when the verse is read in context (1 Cor. 14:1–5), it isn't clear, for several reasons, that the gift of tongues in 1 Corinthians is truly different from the gift in Acts. First, that those in Acts 2 understood the languages spoken doesn't prove that the gift of tongues is different. They understood the tongues because they knew the languages. The problem in 1 Corinthians is that no one was present who knew the languages spoken. It isn't the gift of tongues that was different; the *situation* was different.

Second, Paul actually teaches in 1 Corinthians 14:1–5 that tongues are equivalent to prophecy if interpreted. Since the tongues were understood in Acts 2 (people who knew the languages were there), the tongues constituted prophecy. If the tongues were interpreted in 1 Corinthians, they would be equivalent to prophecy as well. There is no difference. "The person who prophesies is greater than the person who speaks in tongues, unless he interprets so that the church may be built up" (1 Cor. 14:5). If the tongue is interpreted, the person who prophesies doesn't edify the church more than the tongue-speaker because in this case speaking in tongues is equivalent to prophecy.

Third, when Paul says tongues lead to judgment he is speaking of uninterpreted tongues (1 Cor. 14:20–23). But in Acts, the people present *knew the languages* spoken. Paul's very point in 1 Corinthians 14:20–23 is that if people understood the tongues, there would not be judgment. Again, the example doesn't prove that tongues are different, only that the situation was different.

Fourth, we should not argue from Acts that the *only purpose* of tongues is to preach the gospel. Certainly, people could be edified by others praising God when tongues were spoken. Prophetic speech has more than one purpose, and so does the gift of tongues. Actually, Acts itself indicates that there is more than one purpose to tongues. When Cornelius and his friends and the Ephesian twelve spoke in tongues (Acts 10:44–48; 19:1–7), they were not preaching the gospel to Peter and Paul respectively. The gift wasn't functioning in exactly the same as it was in Acts 2. In the case of Cornelius and the Ephesian twelve, they were probably praising God in tongues for their salvation. Different purposes for the gift of tongues says nothing about the nature of the gift of tongues.

There is no compelling evidence, therefore, that Acts and 1 Corinthians refer to two different kinds of gifts of tongues. In both instances, languages with a discernible code are in view. If no interpreters are present, then no one understands what is being said except God. However, if an interpreter is present (either someone who understands the language from birth or someone with the gift of interpretation), then the tongue (i.e., language) is no longer mysterious.

Christopher Forbes has also argued that the word "tongue" (*glōssa*) doesn't refer to ecstatic utterances in Hellenistic literature or in the New Testament but to a meaningful language.[2] Some object by asking, *What is the point of speaking in another language if no one understands what is being said?* But the same objection applies to ecstatic utterances, and thus this isn't really an argument for ecstatic utterances.

Speaking in Tongues Today?

If tongue-speaking refers to speaking human languages and does not consist of ecstatic utterances, what should we make of contemporary tongue-speaking which is clearly ecstatic utterances? Virtually no tongue-speaking today fits the biblical depiction of tongues, since people are not speaking in discernible languages. The contemporary "gift" doesn't match what is in the Scriptures.

What should we make of contemporary tongue-speaking?

It doesn't follow from this that such tongue-speaking is evil or demonic. J. I. Packer may be correct in suggesting that most contemporary tongue-speaking

---

[2] Christopher Forbes, *Prophecy and Inspired Speech in Early Christianity and Its Hellenistic Environment* (WUNT 2/75; Tübingen, Germany: J.C.B. Mohr, 1995), 44–74.

is a form of psychological relaxation.[3] Packer compares it to singing to oneself in the shower, and he isn't trying to insult in saying this.

Thus, contemporaries who say they speak in tongues—like those who say they have the gift of prophecy—aren't actually practicing the biblical gift. Those who think they are prophesying are actually sharing impressions, and those who claim to have the biblical gift of tongues aren't speaking in other languages but in ecstatic utterances. It doesn't follow that what they are doing is necessarily evil, but neither is it the same thing as the gift we find in the Scriptures.

Conclusion

Most argue that what we read about in 1 Corinthians 14 demonstrates that the gift of tongues is different from what we find in Acts, but I have tried to show in this chapter that such an interpretation isn't convincing. What makes Acts and 1 Corinthians different isn't the nature of the gift of tongues but the situation. In Acts, people who knew the languages spoken were present, but in 1 Corinthians tongues were spoken in a situation where people didn't know the languages spoken, and thus an interpreter of tongues was required. It isn't

---

[3] J. I. Packer, *Keep in Step with the Spirit: Finding Fullness in Our Walk with God*, revised and enlarged (Grand Rapids, MI: Baker, 2005), 168–70.

surprising that the gift in Acts and 1 Corinthians is the same, for we would naturally expect that it would be. The burden of proof is on those who argue that the gift is of a different nature in 1 Corinthians.

I have also argued in this chapter that speaking in tongues should be understood as speaking in other languages. Thus, those who speak in ecstatic utterances do not have the biblical gift of tongues.

Discussion Questions

1. What was the significance of the gift of tongues in the book of Acts?

2. Do you think ecstatic utterances and tongues are the same thing? Why or why not?

Chapter Nine

Understanding the Significance
of the Gift of Tongues

We have seen that what many in charismatic churches today consider speaking in tongues is different from the biblical gifts of tongues. We should not assume, as a result, that it is evil or demonic, but it doesn't fit the New Testament's description of the gift. Rather than these ecstatic utterances, the New Testament gift of tongues was a gift of speaking in real human languages, and when interpreted and understood, it was closely linked with prophecy (Acts 2:16–18). Clearly, then, it had an important role in the New Testament church.

Thus, we now turn to an explanation of how the gift of tongues functioned and was supposed to function in the New Testament. We will again look at Acts and 1 Corinthians 12–14 to discern the function of tongues in the New Testament.

The Function of the Gift of Tongues in Acts

We begin with the gift of tongues in Acts, and we can be rather brief, since the texts about tongues in Acts have been considered from various angles already. We saw that the gift of tongues in Acts 2:1–4; 10:44–48; and 19:1–7 was human languages, but we didn't ask why the gift was given.

We consider Pentecost first of all where the 120 were speaking in tongues. We have no antecedent in the Old Testament to speaking in tongues as the 120 did here. Can we discern the reason they spoke in tongues?

Some have said that speaking in tongues evidences the baptism of the Spirit, which is often taken by such adherents to be a subsequent event in the life of a Christian. But we already consider this argument's weaknesses earlier in the book. The baptism of the Spirit at Pentecost doesn't signify subsequence but inauguration—the inauguration of the Christian church and the new covenant, where the gift of the Spirit is poured out on all! Tongue-speaking here functions as a counter to the Tower of Babel account (Gen. 11:1–9) where the languages of human beings were confused. Here we find understanding and communication among people of many different cultures, and this points to and anticipates the new creation that is coming, a world where there are no barriers. The promise of universal blessing, which was first made to Abraham (Gen. 12:3), is becoming a reality at Pentecost. We see here the fulfillment of God's great covenant promises.

In the case of Cornelius and his friends (Acts 10:44–48), the gift of tongues certifies that Gentiles who were not circumcised and did not keep the Old Testament law had truly received the Spirit (Acts 11:17; 15:7–11). Jewish Christians would be suspicious—as Acts 11:1–18 and Acts 15:1–29 testify—about whether Gentiles who were uncircumcised truly belonged to the people of God. But the giving of the very same gift to the Gentiles as to the 120 at Pentecost left no doubt that they too belonged to God's people. In fact, this is the very argument made in Acts 10:45–46. The Jews were astonished that God had poured out the Spirit on Gentiles, but they knew Cornelius and his friends had received the Spirit since they spoke in tongues. Thus, Peter concluded they should be baptized, since they "have received the Holy Spirit just as we have" (Acts 10:47).

We actually don't read that the Samaritans spoke in tongues (Acts 8:4–24), though they probably did since Simon was amazed when he "saw that the Spirit was given through the laying on of the apostles' hands" (Acts 8:18). We don't need to rehearse here the previous discussion on why the Spirit was withheld from the Samaritans until Peter and John laid hands upon them; we can simply say that the speaking of tongues among the Samaritans was indisputable evidence that the ancient enemy of the Jews had truly received the Spirit and belonged to the people of God.

It is more difficult to discern why the Ephesian twelve spoke in tongues (Acts 19:1–7). I argued earlier that they hadn't entered the new age of redemptive history until Paul came and laid hands on them and they received the Spirit. Before that time they had not put their faith in Jesus and had only received John the Baptist's baptism, and thus they couldn't really be counted as Christians. They were, so to speak, living in a redemptive histori-cal time warp, as if Jesus hadn't come at all. Why then did God give the Ephesian twelve the gift of tongues?

The reason might seem to be of little importance to us since we don't think much about John the Baptist. New Testament writers, however, emphasize Jesus' superiority to the Baptist. Luke contrasts Jesus and John the Baptist and shows that Jesus was superior. Jesus' birth was more amazing than John's because the Baptist was born to an old infertile couple, but Jesus was born to a virgin (Luke 1:5–2:7). The Baptist prepared the way for Jesus (Luke 1:76–77), but Jesus is the promised son of David and the fulfillment of all the covenant promises (Luke 1:68–75). The Baptist baptized in water, but Jesus will baptize in the Holy Spirit (Luke 3:16).

Nor is Luke the only writer who emphasizes that Jesus takes precedence over the Baptist. In John's Gospel, we see that the Baptist is a witness (John 1:6–8), but Jesus is the Word of God, and God himself (John 1:1–2, 18). Jesus is the bridegroom, but John is the friend of the bridegroom (John 3:29), and so John is content to "decrease" and to allow Jesus to "increase" (John 3:30).

The story of the Ephesian twelve, then, shows that Jesus, in contrast to John, baptizes with the Spirit, and their speaking in tongues upon receiving the Spirit verifies Jesus' preeminence over the Baptist. Presumably the Gospel of John emphasizes that the Baptist was secondary to Jesus because some were tempted to exalt him over Jesus; Acts 19:1–7 fulfills the same function. All glory belongs to Jesus as the promised one! The Ephesian twelve speak in tongues to verify they had received the Spirit, confirming that Jesus is greater than John the Baptist.

The Function of the Gift of Tongues in 1 Corinthians

When we come to 1 Corinthians 12–14, it is evident that the Corinthians exalted the gift of tongues over all other gifts. The experience of the Spirit coming upon one, causing one to speak to God in a previously unknown language was intoxicating. It seemed like a special indication of God's favor. Paul emphasizes, in response to their fascination with tongues, that all the gifts are important. No one is inferior or superior based on the gift they have. Nor is any particular gift comprehensive. The Corinthians thought that those who had the gift of tongues were part of the spiritual elite, and Paul brings them back to reality.

Prophecy was *functionally* more important than tongues because those gathered could *understand* the prophetic word and were edified by what was said (1 Cor. 14:1–19). When believers spoke in tongues and there was no interpretation, the congregation wasn't strengthened or helped by what was said. Those who spoke in tongues were only concerned with their own experience; they should have considered the benefit to others. Paul argued that their experience was of no benefit at all without an interpreter since no one else could understand or comprehend what they were saying.

We should also remind ourselves of our prior study on the baptism of the Spirit. It is evident that speaking in tongues isn't the sign of Spirit baptism (1 Cor. 12:13) since *all believers* are baptized with the Spirit, but not all believers speak in tongues (1 Cor. 12:30). There is no basis, then, for saying that all believers *should* speak in tongues. Some push against this conclusion, since Paul says, "I wish all of you spoke in other tongues" (1 Cor. 14:5), and "I thank God that I speak in other tongues more than all of you" (1 Cor. 14:18). It is imperative, however, that these two statements be read in context, so that we understand their rhetorical purpose. In 1 Corinthians 14:1–5 prophecy is preferred to tongues because the church is strengthened and helped by prophecies. They are edified by prophecy because they understand what is being said. By the time Paul gets to verse 5 and says that he wishes all spoke in tongues, he adds this comment because he doesn't want the congregation to think that he was actually hostile to speaking in tongues. Since he has emphasized that prophecy is more edifying to the congregation, he doesn't want the Corinthians to overcorrect and think they should shun the gift. Thus, Paul said it would be a good thing if all spoke in tongues, but he didn't realistically think or expect that *all would* or *should* speak in tongues. What Paul says is rhetorical, and we see a similar example of this in 1 Corinthians 7:7 where he says that he wishes all people were single as he was. We know, however, that Paul didn't think all people *should* be single or *would* be single. The same principle applies when we interpret 1 Corinthians 14:5.

Paul's remark that he spoke in tongues more than all of them (1 Cor. 14:18) could also be misunderstood. The comment is tacked onto the end of a section (1 Cor. 14:6–19) where Paul makes a sustained argument *against* uninterpreted tongues. The importance of understanding and comprehensibility is emphasized repeatedly in these verses. Once again, Paul doesn't want the Corinthians to misunderstand; he isn't an opponent of the gift of tongues. He prizes the gift personally since he speaks in tongues regularly. Clearly, Paul doesn't think all should speak in tongues, since he says they should seek and desire the greater gifts. And it is evident from Paul's argument that tongues isn't a greater gift, because it doesn't edify the church to the same extent prophecy does (1 Cor. 12:31; 14:1).

The Corinthians were wrong to overestimate and prize tongues unduly, because all the gifts belong to this present evil age, and none last forever (1 Cor. 13:8). Spiritual gifts don't bring perfection, for "we know in part, and prophesy in part" (1 Cor. 13:9), and when the perfect arrives they will no longer be needed (1 Cor. 13:10). The perfect, as I will argue later, is the second coming of Christ when we will see him "face to face" so now all the gifts, including tongues, belong to the realm of knowing "in part." Paul compares the gifts of the present age to childhood and to becoming an adult (1 Cor. 13:11). The gifts are wonderful and represent God's love to us in the present age, but they will be put away when we reach adulthood (i.e., at the second coming). They will seem like "childish things" compared to the knowledge and experience of God awaiting us. Paul isn't criticizing tongues or any other spiritual gift, but he reminds us that they are not the pinnacle of spiritual experience.

> *Paul isn't criticizing tongues or any other spiritual gift, but he reminds us that they are not the pinnacle of spiritual experience.*

One of the more difficult paragraphs on tongues is the discussion on 1 Corinthians 14:20–25. The readers are exhorted to "be infants in evil" but not to be children in their thinking; they needed to consider matters with the maturity of adults (1 Cor. 14:20). Paul draws from Isaiah 28:11–12 to make his point. Isaiah 28 contains an oracle of judgment against Ephraim, the northern kingdom of Israel. The priests and prophets were indicted for their lack of perception and discernment, but instead of repenting, they ridiculed the judgment pronounced against them and the nation. They mocked the oracles pronounced by Isaiah as if they were baby talk (Isa. 28:9), as if they were the babbling of infants (Isa. 28:10). Isaiah replies that when the Assyrians sweep into Israel—which they did in 722 BC—their language would be as incomprehensible as baby talk, since the Assyrians spoke in another language (Isa. 28:11–12). The language of the Assyrians might sound like baby talk to Israel, but it would signify the judgment of God upon the nation as the nation was sent into exile.

The question we must ask is why Paul uses such an illustration in 1 Corinthians. What's his point? Why does he talk about the judgment inflicted by the Assyrians? We are told in 14:22 that tongues are a "sign, not for believers, but unbelievers." The crucial question is, *How do tongues function as a sign for unbelievers?*

Paul answers that question in verse 23: "If, therefore, the whole church assembles together and all are speaking in other tongues and people who are outsiders or unbelievers come in, will they not say that you are out of your minds?" Tongues are *a sign of judgment* for unbelievers; they lead to judgment because outsiders, when they see believers speaking in tongues, have no idea what's happening. Instead of being drawn near to God, they are driven away from him. They are repelled from the gospel because they think believers are fanatics—as if they were babbling like babies. Paul doesn't want unbelievers to be judged but to be saved, which is why he gives this corrective.

Prophecy, on the other hand, is to be preferred when the congregation gathers, because it has the potential of bringing unbelievers to faith (14:24–25). The unbeliever may hear the words spoken, be convicted of sin, and confess that God's presence is in the congregation. Incidentally, Paul isn't contradicting himself in saying prophecy isn't for unbelievers but believers (14:22). Some think there is a contradiction since he gives an illustration of an unbeliever coming to faith through prophecy (14:24–25)! But Paul's point is that prophecy assists people in their faith, whether they are already believers or hearing the gospel for the first time. The main point regarding tongues in 1 Corinthians 14:20–25 should be restated. Paul isn't hostile to tongues, but in the assembly it should not be practiced if there is not an interpreter, for it may lead unbelievers to reject the gospel. And the congregation gathers for the salvation of the lost, not their judgment!

Rules about Tongues

In 1 Corinthians 14:27–28, Paul sets forth some basic rules regarding speaking in tongues when the congregation is gathered. First of all, only two or three should speak in tongues during the meetings, and the same rule is also applied to prophets (1 Cor. 14:29). Paul is aware that meetings can go too long and be dominated by a single person. Some people think if the Spirit is moving, time should not be a concern, but Paul doesn't agree. Those who are convinced that their spiritual gifts must be expressed when the congregation meets are mistaken.

Second, Paul reminds prophets that their spiritual gifts *can be* and *must be* controlled (1 Cor. 14:32). Those who protest that they can't limit the Spirit when he comes upon them are actually behaving selfishly instead of considering what is edifying for the entire congregation.

Third, gifts must be exercised in an orderly fashion (1 Cor. 14:33, 40). This means that when people speak in tongues, only one person speaks at a time (1 Cor. 14:27). There is no place for overlapping tongues, which would produce a cacophony of languages without any comprehension. Paul rules out charismatic chaos, for charismatic gifts and order and peace aren't enemies, but friends. Supernatural realities and orderly meetings are not a contradiction but express the way the Spirit works in the congregation.

Further, if there isn't an interpreter present, those with the gift of tongues should refrain from speaking in tongues in the congregation (1 Cor. 14:28). Apparently those who spoke in tongues were either able to interpret their own tongue, or they should know if someone with the gift of interpretation was present in the congregation. We see here as well that Paul has no problem with private tongue-speaking. We wish we knew more about why Paul thinks private tongue-speaking is helpful if there is no interpreter, but he doesn't elaborate on this point, for he isn't really concerned in this letter with matters of private worship. Paul clearly allows, however, private tongue-speaking. If the person with the gift of tongues can't speak in the assembled meeting, he or she can "speak to himself and to God" (1 Cor. 14:28). They are free to exercise that gift in private in God's presence. Paul recognizes that a person speaking in tongues privately may edify himself (1 Cor. 14:4). It is almost certain that Paul spoke privately in tongues since he claimed that he spoke in tongues more than all of them (1 Cor. 14:18).

But private tongue-speaking obviously is not necessary for spiritual growth and sanctification! We know this because not all believers speak in tongues, nor should they (1 Cor. 12:30). Actually, private tongue-speaking comes up as an aside in 1 Corinthians 12–14, and the subject isn't elaborated on because it really isn't important. Still, the private experience can be a blessing and Paul has no quarrel with it.

Conclusion

The gift of tongues has more than one purpose, and the fact that it has more than one purpose says nothing about whether the gift is different in 1 Corinthians from what we find in Acts. We see in Acts that tongues are given to signify the arrival of the new creation at Pentecost. Gentiles, the Samaritans, and the Ephesian twelve are given the gift of tongues to certify that they have truly received the Spirit, showing that they are truly part of the people of God. It doesn't follow that all believers who have the Spirit speak in tongues. These groups spoke in tongues because there would have been some question about their inclusion in the people of God, and the gift of tongues demonstrated clearly that they belonged to God.

Tongue-speaking in the church must be edifying, according to 1 Corinthians, and it only edifies if it is interpreted. Thus, tongue-speaking is not allowed when the church is gathered unless there is an interpreter. People are only edified when they *understand* what is going on. If unbelievers come into the congregation, and there is tongue-speaking without an interpretation, they will think believers are spiritual fanatics and reject the Christian faith. Paul wants the meeting structured so that unbelievers are encouraged to put their faith in Jesus.

Along the same lines, there is no place for everyone speaking in tongues all at once, because people don't comprehend what is going on in the midst of a cacophony of voices. Tongue-speaking should be limited to one person at a time, and there must be an interpreter. Paul restricts how many people in the congregation can speak in tongues, for the entire meeting must not be dominated by tongue-speaking (or by prophecy either, for that matter).

We can apply a principle from this to all of the spiritual gifts God gives. Unless they are exercised in an orderly way, and unless they build up the congregation, we shouldn't exercise them. In this way, Paul makes clear that the emphasis of spiritual gifts is not on individuals, but on the church. We must remember as we gather with our churches that it's not about us as individuals. We don't go to church to consume but to serve and to worship together.

Discussion Questions

1. What is the relationship of tongues and prophecy in the Bible? Based on that relationship, do you think the gift of tongues is still active?

2. Paul makes clear that speaking in tongues is not the pinnacle of Christian experience. Did that cause him to criticize the gift?

3. What can we learn from Paul's response to the Corinthians's obsession with the gift of tongues?

4. How can we apply the principle of Paul's instructions about tongues to all the spiritual gifts?

Chapter Ten

Unconvincing Arguments for Cessation of the Gifts

When it comes to spiritual gifts, believers disagree today on whether all the gifts still exist. Some are continuationists, arguing that virtually all the gifts still exist today. Others are open but cautious about whether certain gifts still exist. Still others are cessationists, arguing that certain gifts have ceased. Here we will consider very briefly two different arguments for the cessation of some of the gifts and argue that both of them are unconvincing.

"The Perfect" Is the Bible or Spiritual Maturity

I begin with the most common version, which is particularly found in dispensational circles. The claim is that the supernatural gifts will cease with the writing of the New Testament, and the argument is made from 1 Corinthians 13:8–12. We see in verse 8 that the gifts won't last forever. "But as for prophecies, they will come to an end; as for tongues, they will cease; as for knowledge, it will come to an end." Some have argued that the particular verb with tongues as the subject is significant. Tongues "will cease" (*pausontai*), whereas prophecy and knowledge "will come to an end" (*katargēthēsetai*). The argument is that the middle voice with the verb *pausontai* ("will cease") shows that tongues will cease in and of themselves. Of course, one could also argue that the verbs are synonyms and still see the gifts coming to an end before the second coming.

The key feature of this argument is that the gifts will end when "the perfect comes" (1 Cor. 13:10). On this view, many of the gifts (such as tongues) end when the New Testament is completed, when the canon of Scripture is completed. At that point some of the spiritual gifts are no longer needed, since in the New Testament we have God's perfect revelation. A variant of this view is that the perfect doesn't refer to the writing of the New Testament but to spiritual maturity. Spiritual gifts are no longer necessary because now that we have the New Testament we have all we need for spiritual maturity.

The Perfect Is the Second Coming

The arguments for cessationism from 1 Corinthians 13:8–10 aren't exegetically convincing for a number of reasons. First, those who appeal to the difference in the verbs put too much weight on the grammatical difference. The two different verbs "come to an end" (*katargeō*) and "cease" (*pauomai*) are used for stylistic variety, and we should not press any distinction between the two verbs. I am not saying that the verbs are absolutely synonymous, but that we shouldn't read into them a major distinction.

The key to resolving the interpretation of 1 Corinthians 13:8–12 is what Paul means by the coming of "the perfect" (*to teleion*). We have seen that some understand "the perfect" to refer to spiritual maturity, but it is scarcely evident that Christians are more mature post-canonically. It isn't clear, in other words, that we are more mature than Christians were in the first century. Such a claim is a rather bold assertion, for it could be read to say that we are even more spiritually mature than the apostles. A quick reading of church history and of the current evangelical landscape raises significant doubts about the assertion as well.

A significant problem with seeing "the perfect" as the completed canon is the historical location of Paul when he wrote 1 Corinthians. He certainly believed that his words in 1 Corinthians were authoritative and represented God's word

to his readers (1 Cor. 14:37–38). Indeed, Paul's authority per-
meates all his letters (cf. 1 Thess. 2:13; 2 Thess. 3:14). Reading
letters orally in the congregation signified their authority, and
Paul enjoins recipients to read his letters (Col. 4:16; 1 Thess.
5:27). Nevertheless, God didn't reveal to Paul that he was writing letters that would be collected in a New Testament canon.
Yes, Paul knew his letters were authoritative, but he had no
vision that history would last a long time and that his letters
would be collected with other New Testament writings that
would function as the authority for churches down through
history. Instead, Paul believed Jesus would return soon, and
history would come to an end. This isn't to take away from
Paul's authority or accuracy, for nothing he wrote is contradicted by two thousand years of history passing. The point I
am making is that it is almost impossible that Paul could have
meant by "the perfect" the New Testament canon.

Not only is it unlikely that Paul was referring to the canon
when he speaks of "the perfect" coming, it is even more unlikely
that the Corinthians would have understood the word *perfect*
this way. Let's say, for the sake of argument, that Paul is referring to the New Testament canon. The problem that immediately emerges is that there is no way that the Corinthians
would have understood what Paul was talking about! Paul
would have had to explain in much more detail than he does
here that by "the perfect" he had in mind the completion of the
New Testament. Certainly, the Corinthians never imagined or

dreamt of a New Testament canon. And why would Paul write about such an idea to them since many—probably most—of them wouldn't live to see the canon completed, and even if they did live that long, the canon wasn't compiled together? Indeed, if this is what Paul had in mind, the Corinthians would then know that Jesus could not and would not return for a number of years, and he would only come when the New Testament was finished and accepted as authoritative.

If we look at the context of 1 Corinthians 13:8–12, the coming of "the perfect" brings what is "partial" to an end (13:10). Paul says that now we "know in part, but then I will know fully, as I am fully known" (13:12). Presently, our knowledge is incomplete, and "we see only a reflection as in a mirror," but then we will see "face to face" (13:12). It is clear, therefore, that "the perfect" is another way of describing "face to face," and seeing "face to face" most naturally refers to Christ's second coming. Understanding "the perfect" to refer to Jesus' coming is something the Corinthians would clearly understand, and also fits with the emphasis on Jesus' second coming in Paul's theology.

The phrase "face to face" echoes theophanies in the Old Testament, instances where God appeared to human beings so that they encountered him. When Jacob wrestled with the Angel of the Lord, he saw God "face to face." Gideon feared that he was going to die since he saw the angel of the Lord "face to face" (Judg. 6:22). Moses was incomparable as a prophet because the Lord knew him "face to face" (Deut. 34:10; cf. Deut. 5:4).

The idiom "face to face" in 1 Corinthians 13:12 doesn't suggest something abstract like the New Testament canon or spiritual maturity. Instead, it represents the language of encounter with God, and so naturally refers to the second coming, since we will see Jesus "face to face" when "the perfect comes" (1 Cor. 13:10).

The notion that "the perfect" refers to the canon or to spiritual maturity is also ruled out by what is said about knowledge. "When the perfect comes, the partial will come to an end" (1 Cor. 13:10). Now Paul sees imperfectly and knows partially, but when the perfect arrives he will see "face to face" (1 Cor. 13:12). Partial knowledge will give way to complete knowledge (1 Cor. 13:12). If the "perfect" refers to the New Testament canon or to spiritual maturity, we no longer have partial knowledge. Those who have the canon or those who are mature know fully. Indeed, they know more than Paul who confesses that he knows only partially! But any notion that our knowledge is perfect or better than Paul's is clearly false. Our knowledge continues to be imperfect. We know truly but not comprehensively and exhaustively. We will only know fully when Jesus returns, when we see him face to face.

We will only know fully when Jesus returns, when we see him face to face.

Conclusion

We have seen that arguments from 1 Corinthians 13:8–12 for the cessation of the gifts fail. The "perfect" doesn't refer to the New Testament canon or to spiritual maturity but to the second coming of Christ. If anything, Paul teaches that the spiritual gifts persist and last until the second coming. In fact, I think this is the best argument for the spiritual gifts continuing until today. And I understand why some readers may disagree with me on this very point. As I said in the introduction, I could be mistaken in arguing for cessationism. Nonetheless, I still think cessationism is true, and I turn to the reasons for this judgment in the next chapter.

Discussion Questions

1. What is "the perfect" in 1 Corinthians 13?

2. How does the knowledge that we will not know fully until Christ returns inform our lives?

3. What does it tell us about the nature of spiritual gifts that they will end when Christ returns?

Chapter Eleven

An Argument for Cessationism

We have seen in 1 Corinthians 13:8–12 that some arguments for cessationism are unconvincing, and that a good argument can be made for all the gifts continuing until the second coming. We see from 1 Corinthians 13:8–12 why many find such a view to be convincing. Indeed, they may think that any argument for cessation of the gifts is forced. If 1 Corinthians 13:8–12 were the only relevant text on the matter, then I would agree that all the gifts continue until Jesus returns. I would suggest that other texts, however, cast doubt on whether 1 Corinthians 13:8–12 *requires* that all the gifts continue until Jesus returns, and thus suggest that "the gifts" as they are practiced today in most churches are not the same thing as the gifts described in the New Testament.

Let me reiterate what I said in the last chapter. Paul believed Jesus was coming soon, and he said that gifts would end when Jesus returned. What wasn't clearly revealed to Paul is that history would last at least two thousand more years (though nothing he wrote contradicted this notion). The next point is speculative and could be off-center, but the Lord didn't reveal clearly to Paul that the gifts would end because he didn't want the Corinthians or Paul to know the day of his coming! Every generation should live as if it is the last generation, and the Lord keeps us on our toes, and we rightly say, "Jesus is coming soon!" But if Paul taught that some of the gifts would slowly cease, then it would be evident to both Paul and the Corinthians that Jesus would not and could not come during their lifetime.

The point for the Corinthians and for us in 1 Corinthians 13:8–12 is that the gifts would not persist in the new creation; they are not the pinnacle of biblical revelation. I suggest that though 1 Corinthians 13:8–12 tells us the gifts will end when Christ returns, it doesn't require that all the gifts last until Jesus returns.

Many Christians throughout history have rightly discerned from Scripture, theological deduction, and experience that at least some of the gifts have ceased. The Lord did not choose to divulge the particulars to Paul and to the Corinthians in 1 Corinthians 13:8–12 because the issue wasn't relevant to their lives. They lived in the first generation after all. All of this is to say that whether the gifts persist has to be established on other grounds, grounds that can be defended both biblically and theologically.

The Foundational Role of Apostles

The basis for cessationism is the claim that the church was "built on the foundation of the apostles and prophets" (Eph. 2:20). We saw earlier that the prophets here are New Testament prophets. The word *apostleship* is used in a technical sense here, and Paul doesn't have in mind pioneer missionaries. Actually, many continuationists are cessationists when it comes to apostleship, for they also believe that the gift of apostleship in the technical sense has passed away.

In the New Testament, the Twelve were called as apostles (cf. Matt. 10:2; Luke 6:13), with Matthias replacing Judas as the twelfth apostle (Acts 1:15–26).[1] The foundational gift of apostleship wasn't limited to the Twelve. Paul was clearly an apostle of Jesus Christ (e.g., Rom. 1:1; 1 Cor. 9:1; 2 Cor. 1:1; etc.). James the half-brother of Jesus is also identified as an apostle (Gal. 1:19). Further, we see that Barnabas, along with Paul, is designated as an apostle in Acts (Acts 14:4, 14). Perhaps a few others were apostles as well.

---

[1] The notion that a mistake was made in selecting the twelfth apostle is itself mistaken. For a convincing exposition, see Eckhard Schnabel, *Acts* (ZECNT; Grand Rapids, MI: Zondervan, 2012), 90–107.

Now that the foundation of the church has been laid, we no longer have authoritative apostles like the Twelve, Paul, James, etc. Roman Catholics, of course, see apostolic teaching as continuing with the Pope. Evangelicals, however, rightly believe that the apostolic office is not transmitted through human beings. Apostolic authority is enshrined in the Scriptures, in the canon. The Scriptures constitute our sole and final authority, and the teaching of the apostles is preserved in the scriptural witness (Acts 2:42). When James died in Acts 12, he wasn't replaced as an apostle, showing that the gift of apostleship didn't continue in subsequent generations. To qualify as an apostle, one had to be commissioned as an apostle and to see the risen Lord. Jesus Christ appeared to Paul on the Damascus Road and summoned him to apostolic service (Acts 9:1–19; 1 Cor. 9:1–2; Gal. 1:13–17). In 1 Corinthians 15:8 Paul sees himself as the *last* person Jesus appeared to, showing that there would be no apostles appointed after the apostle Paul.

> *Apostolic authority is enshrined in the Scriptures.*

As I mentioned, even many continuationists believe that the gift of apostleship has ended. So, they are cessationists of a sort as well! Those groups that think apostles are still around open themselves up to the danger of authoritarianism, where certain leaders are virtually given a cultic status. Such authoritarianism represses critical thinking and opens the door to abuse. We see such an abuse of authority in the case of Diotrophes who imposes his will on those under his leadership (3 John 9–10). Most evangelicals agree that no human beings have the authority of the original apostles, and the distinctive authority of the apostles is preserved in the New Testament.

The Foundational Role of Prophets

Many, then, would agree that the gift of apostleship has passed away. But what about prophets? We have seen the church is "built on the foundation of the apostles and prophets" (Eph. 2:20). Prophets, along with apostles, played a key role in the founding and establishing of the church. I have argued earlier in this book that prophets infallibly spoke the word of God. The words of prophets were not mixed with error, but were like the words of Old Testament prophets—authoritative and true.

The definition of prophecy is crucial to the argument made here. If the prophecies of New Testament prophets could be mixed with error, then I would have no quarrel with New Testament prophets existing today. We would then have the task of discerning where they speak truth and where they err. This poses a significant problem, however because if New Testament prophecy is mixed with error, discriminating which prophets are true and which prophets are false becomes much more difficult. What set me personally back on the road to cesssationism is this very matter of prophecy. I slowly became convinced that the idea that New Testament prophets were different in nature from Old Testament prophets was flawed. Instead, it is more convincing to say that New Testament prophets were infallible like Old Testament prophets.

Saying that New Testament prophets spoke infallibly like Old Testament prophets fits well the conception that the church is built upon the foundation of the apostles and prophets. Both the apostles and New Testament prophets, in other words, spoke the authoritative and infallible word of God. Now if such authoritative apostles don't exist today (and many continuationists agree on this point), and if prophets spoke infallible words like the apostles, and if the church is built on the foundation of the apostles and prophets, then there are good grounds to conclude that the gift of prophecy has ceased as well. Since prophecy is defined here as speaking the infallible word of God and since the church is built on the foundation of the apostles and prophets, there are no longer prophets today, since the foundation of the church has been laid. The sole and final authority of Scripture is threatened if so-called prophets today give revelations which have the same authority as Scripture.

> *The sole and final authority of Scripture is threatened if so-called prophets today give revelations which have the same authority as Scripture.*

If one adopts this definition of prophecy, for anyone to claim such a gift of prophecy today would constitute a threat and danger to the church. Such claims would compromise the unique authority of Scripture, and the potential for spiritual abuse and a cultic type of authoritarianism would be great.

Perhaps the gift of prophecy existed for a few hundred years in the early church, since it took some time for the church to agree upon the settled canon of Scripture. We can't, then, fix a definite date for the cessation of prophecy. The gift slowly and gradually faded away, while the New Testament canon was being settled and later widely accepted. The same could possibly be said for some of the other gifts as well. Perhaps (it is hard to be certain) they functioned for some time as the church transitioned to a stage where the canonical Scriptures took root.[2]

---

[2] Vern Poythress suggests that gifts like prophecy no longer operate the way they did in the New Testament, and what we see in the case of prophecy (and some other gifts) is analogous to what we see in the New Testament. Such a suggestion is helpful in that Poythress recognizes that what people call prophecy today isn't the same gift that we find in the New Testament. Poythress is a cessationist in saying that at least some of the gifts don't operate the way they did in the New Testament, and this is another way of saying some of the gifts don't exist today. Or, at least they don't exist insofar as they don't match the New Testament definition of the gift. The plus in Poythress's explanation also has a minus at the same time since the "gifts" he sees operating now aren't anchored directly in Scripture. They are only analogous to what we see in the Scriptures. For instance, the way we use the word *prophecy* today doesn't match what the New Testament means by

The view argued for here could be called nuanced cessationism. I am not claiming that all the gifts have *necessarily*
passed away. The point is that, since the church is founded
upon the apostles and prophets, apostles and prophets are no
longer functioning today. Perhaps some reading this book will
want to take my argument only this far: we no longer have
the gifts of apostleship and prophecy. The Scriptures constitute
our sole and final authority, and thus the role the apostles and
prophets played in the foundational period of the church is no
longer needed. The Scriptures are our sole and final authority.

The Role of Tongues, Healing, and Miracles

It seems to me that the role of other gifts that are ques-
tioned is not as important. I am thinking particularly of the
gift of tongues, the interpretation of tongues, and healing and

---

prophecy according to Poythress. Thus "gifts" are being practiced for
which there is no New Testament warrant and definition since these
gifts, according to Poythress, aren't the same that we see in Scripture.
It is difficult to see how such a halfway house can be sustained since
the gifts as they are practiced today aren't anchored to the biblical text.
In other words, can we really say that these analogous gifts are rooted
in the scriptural witness if they aren't the same thing we find in the
Scriptures? At a practical level Poythress has suggested a solution that
recognizes some of the strengths in the charismatic movement, and in
many ways his view isn't different from what is argued for here. Still,
we need to see biblical warrant for the idea that the gifts we have today
are still gifts if they are not the same phenomenon we see in the New
Testament.

miracles. Perhaps tongues still exists today, but I am doubtful, since what most practice today is ecstatic utterances, and the gift, as I understand it, is speaking in human languages. It isn't apparent that believers are being given this latter gift today; if they are, it seems to be exceedingly rare.

Another argument for tongues ceasing is the claim that interpreted tongues (which is the only kind of tongues which should be practiced in the congregation) is equivalent to prophecy. If interpreted tongues are another form of prophecy, and if prophecy has ceased, then there are good reasons to think tongues have ceased as well. The notion that an interpreted tongue is equivalent to prophecy is clearly supported in 1 Corinthians 14:5. The close relationship between comprehensible tongues and prophecy is also found in Acts 2. In fact, Luke tells us that interpreted tongues are prophecy. When the 120 speak in tongues and they are understood by those in Jerusalem (Acts 2:1–13), it is clear from Acts 2:17–18 that such interpreted tongues are defined as prophesying.

Interpreted tongues, then, proclaim the word of God just as prophecy does. If interpreted tongues are another form of prophecy, it would make sense that they no longer exist today, since they have the same function as prophecy.

Perhaps some find such an argument unconvincing. My case doesn't depend upon it. The role of tongues isn't as important if there are no claims to new revelation. If one separates tongues from prophecy, then there is no new revelation through tongues. But then one wonders what function interpreted tongues actually play in the congregation if the word shared doesn't reveal God's truth.

How should we think about miracles and healings?[3] Once again, the problem isn't as significant since there are no claims to new revelation. I tend to think that these gifts don't exist today. If a person has a gift of healing, it seems there would be a pattern of healing. And the healings should be on the same level that we see in the New Testament: healing of the blind, of those who are unable to walk, of those who are deaf, and of those who are near death. Claims to healing are often quite subjective: colds, the flu, stomach and back ailments, sports injuries, etc. Now, I am not denying that God may heal in such instances, and we thank God for it! The issue is that it is often difficult to verify that a miracle has truly taken place. It isn't clear to me that particular people have a *gift* of healing or miracles.

This certainly does not mean there aren't miracles today! God can still heal and do miracles according to his will, and he does! Cessationism doesn't mean there are no miracles in the present age, nor does it mean that we don't pray for healings or miracles. I pray for them regularly. But charismatics must show

---

[3] It is even more difficult to know if people have the gift of faith and distinguishing of spirits. It isn't clear to me that people exercise these gifts but maybe they do. I am quite uncertain about these.

that miracles are really happening to the same extent today as in the New Testament, and that there are people who have the gift of healings and miracles. Many of us believe God can and does work miracles today, but do we have people with the gift of miracles and healing? Is this truly a regular and normative feature in the lives of our churches? I think not. If a continuationist says that the gifts are operating today but to a far inferior degree than what we see in the New Testament, then they seem to be saying that the gifts aren't operating as they did in the New Testament. But how do they know that? The argument actually sounds like a form of cessationism to me.

Cessationism doesn't mean there are no miracles in the present age, nor does it mean that we don't pray for healings or miracles.

Yes, God works miracles, but they are relatively rare. Perhaps God is pleased in cutting-edge missionary situations to grant the same signs and wonders we see in the New Testament era. I think this is certainly possible, and that is why I call my view a nuanced cessationism. Still, we must be on guard about exaggerated stories. It isn't wrong to check out whether a miracle truly occurred. People carefully verified the healing of the blind man in John 9. Christians can be as credulous and superstitious as unbelievers. I have heard some pretty wild stories (not limited to charismatic phenomena) from Christians during my forty-plus years as a believer. Checking out stories doesn't mean that we lack faith. People make all sorts of unsubstantiated claims in life, and it isn't wrong or unbelieving to ask for evidence for an alleged miracle or healing. Yes, God heals. Yes, let's ask God to heal. But let's also recognize that often God doesn't heal, and we don't want to raise false expectations in people about what God will do. The stories of those who aren't healed can be quietly forgotten, but God shows his grace in sustaining them as well. Dramatic healings are the exception (for which we praise God!), and not the rule.

I believe God gave gifts and miracles, signs and wonders, in remarkable ways at certain points in redemptive history to authenticate his revelation. We see this in the Exodus, in the plagues which afflicted Egypt and in the wonderful deliverance of Israel from Egypt. Another high point was present in the era of Elijah and Elisha when Israel was tempted to follow Baal rather than Yahweh. Remarkable signs and wonders under the ministry of Elijah and Elisha attested that Yahweh is God (1 Kings 17–2 Kings 9).

The high point in biblical revelation, of course, is the ministry, death, and resurrection of Jesus Christ. His ministry and the ministry of his followers (especially, but not only, the apostles) were characterized by signs and wonders. I think their primary purpose was to accredit divine revelation in Christ, to signify that Jesus is the new David, the Son of Man, and the Son of God (Heb. 2:4). Other purposes exist when there are miracles as well; they encourage and comfort those healed and bring great joy to God's people. And miracles aren't limited to such high points in redemptive history, as any careful reading of the Old Testament shows, but they are clustered at central eras in the Scriptures. Miracles are an anticipation of the new creation that is coming! God can and does heal when he wills, but the point is that miracles were especially prominent at key turning points in redemptive history.

Now that the church has the authoritative guidance for faith and practice in the Scriptures, the gifts and miracles which were needed to build up the early church are no longer needed, and they are not common. This is not to say, however, that God never does miracles today.

Last, I think it is significant that the great teachers whom God used to bring about the Protestant Reformation were cessationists. Naturally they could be wrong and mistaken. They were fallible just as we are. I don't think, however, that they were quenching the Holy Spirit. They would have loved to see signs and wonders and miracles like there were in the apostolic age. They were cessationists because of their understanding of the Scriptures, and because they operated with definitions of spiritual gifts which are similar to what I have argued for in this book. They were not perfect, but they were right about many things, and we should not be quick to depart from their perspective.

Conclusion

I have argued in this chapter that the gifts of apostle and prophet are no longer functioning, since the church is "built on the foundation of the apostles and prophets" (Eph. 2:20), and that foundation is now established. We now have apostolic and prophetic teaching in the completed canon of the Scriptures. The apostles and New Testament prophets are not on the scene today. New Testament prophets spoke authoritatively and truly and without error, and such prophets don't exist today. If people think such infallible prophets exist today, the final and sole authority of the Scriptures is threatened.

It is more difficult to discern whether gifts like tongues, healing, and miracles exist today. Perhaps God is pleased to grant them in some situations, especially cutting-edge missionary contexts. It seems, however, that gifts like miracles and healings aren't a regular or normative feature of church life. I certainly believe God can perform miracles and does perform miracles today, but such miracles are relatively rare and not the norm. We should pray for healing and for God to act, but we should not create a false assumption that God will always or even regularly heal. Rather, we should trust that he is good, whether he heals or not.

Discussion Questions

1. "Apostolic authority is enshrined in the Scriptures" (p. 158). How does this inform our theology of spiritual gifts?

2. What is the sole and final authority for the Christian life?

3. Can God still perform miracles today?

4. What are some of the most important and impactful things you have learned about spiritual gifts in this book?

Epilogue

As we conclude, it is important to remember that spiritual gifts are not a first-order matter. Those who agree on first-order issues may differ on whether gifts like prophecy and tongues and healing exist today. Still, we agree on the most important questions, such as the authority of Scripture, the person of Jesus Christ, the doctrine of the Trinity, justification by faith alone, etc. As evangelicals, we need to continue to grow in our ability to have loving discussions on where we differ without demonizing one another and without suggesting that those who disagree are somehow less spiritually mature. We see in our culture today that civil discourse is in short supply, and we can stand out as lights by disagreeing in ways that are charitable and kind.

I remind the reader about what I said at the beginning. My perspective could be mistaken, and those who are continuationists may see things more clearly than I. Still, a case has been made in this book for a nuanced cessationism. The key verse for this notion is that the church is "built on the foundation of the apostles and prophets" (Eph. 2:20). Since that apostolic foundation has been laid, apostles and prophets are no longer functioning today. One of the fundamental bases for this judgment is that New Testament prophecy is without error and wholly true. There was a great danger in the New Testament from false prophets, and if the message of New Testament prophets could be mixed with error, it would be remarkably difficult to sort out who was a false prophet and who was a true prophet. Other arguments were also given to support the idea that New Testament prophets were infallible like Old Testament prophets. Such prophets no longer function today, and we have the authoritative and inerrant Scriptures to guide us.

Many other truths and practical applications regarding the gifts have been discussed in this short book. We have seen that gifts are not for our private enjoyment but for the edification and building up of the church of Jesus Christ. Gifts aren't me-centered but others-centered. They are given so that the church will become more and more like her Lord, Jesus Christ. Paul especially emphasizes that love (1 Cor. 13) is far more important than any spiritual gift. When we examine a controversial topic, we are apt to forget this truth. Thus, it is good to end this book by saying, "If I have the right view of spiritual gifts, but I don't have love, then I am nothing."